Paper&Fabric Mache

Paper & Fabric Mache

100 Imaginative & Ingenious Projects to Make

Dawn Cusick

A Sterling/Lark Book
Sterling Publishing Co., Inc. New York

Photography: Evan Bracken, Light Reflections
Art Director: Kathleen Holmes
Production: Elaine Thompson
Proofreading: Julie Brown
Illustrations: Charlie Covington

Library of Congress Cataloging-in-Publication Data

   Paper & fabric mache : 100 imaginative & ingenious projects
to make / Dawn Cusick.
      p.   cm.
   "A Sterling/Lark book."
   Includes bibliographical references and index.
   ISBN 0-8069-0608-1
   1. Papier-mâché.   2. Textile crafts.   I. Title.   II. Title: Paper
and fabric mache.   III. Title: Fabric mache.
TT871.C87   1994
745.54'2--dc20   93-38489
                                                                    CIP

10 9 8 7 6 5 4 3 2

A Sterling/Lark Book

First paperback edition published in 1995 by
Sterling Publishing Company, Inc.
387 Park Avenue South, New York, N.Y. 10016

Produced by Altamont Press, Inc.
50 College Street, Asheville, NC 28801

© 1994 by Altamont Press

Distributed in Canada by Sterling Publishing
   % Canadian Manda Group, One Atlantic Avenue, Suite 105
   Toronto, Ontario, Canada M6K 3E7
Distributed in Great Britain and Europe by Cassell PLC
   Villiers House, 41/47 Strand, London WC2N 5JE, England
Distributed in Australia by Capricorn Link (Australia) Pty Ltd.
   P.O. Box 6651, Baulkham Hills, Business Centre, NSW 2153, Australia

Printed and bound in Hong Kong by Regent Publishing
All rights reserved

Sterling ISBN 0-8069-0608-1 Trade
              0-8069-0609-X Paper

Contents

Contributing Designers

Lucas Adams works in many mediums, including paper-mache, bronze, welded metal, and composite construction. As a child, Lucas lived in the native homes of both his parents (Greece and Mississippi), and he attributes his childhood surroundings with many of his current works.

Avis Wright Everett's first craft experience was stenciling her home in traditional motifs, and she later developed a technique for decorating baskets with stiffened bows made from designer fabrics. Avis has authored several how-to booklets for Plaid Enterprises, Inc., the makers of Stiffy® fabric stiffener.

Fred Tyson Gaylor taught art in the public school system for ten years before changing careers to showroom and movie set design. He is currently a product designer for Hanfords, Inc., a wholesale holiday accessory company in Charlotte, North Carolina.

Marie-Helene Grabman is a former television news writer/producer who now owns a small Scherenschnitte (German papercutting) business. She shares her papercutting art through exhibits, lectures, and publications.

Sarah Kim, originally from Korea, has been creating and selling jewelry and small craft items from ceramic clay for many years, and has just recently discovered that she can achieve many of the same results with instant paper-mache with far less cost.

Anne McCloskey is a freelance artist and designer living in Copley, Ohio. She specializes in wearable art and painting crafts, and especially likes designing for holiday celebrations. Anne experiments with other craft mediums because they provide her with inspiration for her wearable art.

Dolly Lutz Morris lives in rural Pennsylvania with her husband, Bill, and five children. Her shop, 219 Market Square, carries a wide selection of her paper-mache pieces along with her dried flower arrangements and painted furniture. For a catalog of Dolly's work, send a self-addressed business-sized envelope to 219 Market Square, Meadville, PA, 16335.

Mary Beth Ruby, of Bellefonte, Pennsylvania, began sculpting as a child, when her favorite projects ranged from detailed Egyptian cities to space ships with aliens inside. Today she creates paper-mache animals, figurines, bowls, and jewelry. She creates commissioned works and frequently exhibits her sculptures in one-person and juried shows.

Dottie Shultz is a decorative artist living in Dillsburg, Pennsylvania. She is primarily a painter, and specializes in door harps, novelty paintings, and seasonal paper-mache projects though her business, Shultz's Brush and Saw.

Diane Weaver enjoys creating decorative crafts that utilize her true love — painting. She and husband Dick own Gourmet Gardens, an herb nursery and specialty shop in Weaverville, North Carolina. She is the author of Painted Furniture and coauthor of Glorious Christmas Crafts.

Also Thanks to . . .
Joyce Connolly, Darlene Conti, Joyce Cusick, Richard Glass, Doris Neisler, Deanne Nesbit, Laura Rogers and her 5th and 6th grade Spanish classes at Clyde Elementary School, North Carolina. Pamela Schaeffer, Diane Shelton, Bobby Wells, and Mary Ellen Williams.

Also thanks to the people and businesses who shared their modeling talents and products . . .
Sara Allen, Amanda Connolly, Samantha VanderMeade, Nancy McCauley, Mark Mull, Sashi Wald, Barney Wald, Activa Products (instant paper-mache), and Plaid Enterprises, Inc. (Stiffy® fabric stiffener).

Introduction

Paper-mache suffers from a bad reputation in the art and craft fields, the unfortunate victim of malicious rumors and vivid memories from many crafter's pasts of messy, gangly projects. My first paper-mache project was a bracelet, made as a Girl Scout project for points toward a merit badge. I remember loving the fresh smell of the flour and water mache paste, and feeling inspired by how easy it was to make something special. The finished bracelet was less than inspiring, though, and the smell of the flour paste would stay on my arm long after I removed the bracelet.

Unfortunately, I didn't know then what Texas designer Lucas Adams recently explained to me, that these are very forgiving mediums. If you make a mistake, it's so easy to fix. With instant paper-mache, you just use sandpaper or a screw driver to chisel away the area you're unhappy with, apply a fresh layer of mache, and try again. With fabric mache, you just soak the uncooperative area in a little water, add some more stiffening medium, and reshape. With paper and fabric mache, every learning experience can lead to a beautiful, finished project, compared to many other crafts, where your first projects are usually hidden in the very back of the closet. With many crafts, indulging that portion of yourself is

doomed from the start, because the level of technical accomplishment needed to create something lovely to look at is way too difficult for the novice to be successful at first, and we usually surrender in disappointment.

The projects in this book represent a wide range of styles. As you browse through the pages trying to choose a project to make, try to look at the projects as more than just ideas to copy; try to see them as inspirations, as ideas you can adapt to fit your own lifestyle and tastes. If you're intrigued with the elephant head on page 59 but don't believe it will fit in with your current decor, why not use the same instructions to make a replica of your family pet? If you adore the hat on page 93 but bright colors aren't your forte, then just make one from a pastel fabric.

A special thanks needs to be mentioned here to all the designers who contributed their time and creative energy to help create this book. Some are serious artists who just happened to choose paper or fabric mache as their medium, while others are leisure-time crafters who just enjoy making pretty things to brighten other people's lives. All of them, though, are very special people, and it's been great fun working with them.

Paper-Mache Techniques

Paper-mache began almost 2,000 years ago in ancient China as a form of recycling, where scraps of precious handmade paper were made into lacquered helmets to be used as armor. In recent decades, paper-mache was thought of almost exclusively as being made from torn strips of newspaper that had been dipped in a stiffening mixture. Instant paper-mache, though, which has been on the market for more than 20 years, has recently surpassed the newsprint and glue alternative with most crafters.

Instant paper-mache is a powdered paper pulp that has been combined with a glue binder. It's available in craft and art stores, and crafters have the choice of white or gray. If you plan to paint your finished project, there's no need to pay extra for the white. After being mixed with water, instant paper-mache can be molded, sculpted, or sandpapered. The mache is ideal for novices — if you don't like the way the finished project looks, just add another layer of mache and try again. Or try your hand at sculpting and remove some of the areas with a knife. The worst that can happen is that you won't like the piece and will have to add another layer of mache and try again. Crafters who enjoy newspaper macheing (see page 87 for newspaper techniques and recipes) may want to form the base of their projects from newspaper and then top it with a layer of instant mache to for a smoother, more sculptable finished surface area.

Crafting with instant paper-mache requires few tools. A lazy Susan is helpful when working on larger, three-dimensional pieces, although an old plate that you can turn to see all sides of your piece will work just as well. If you fall in love with the medium and plan to work with it a lot, a set of clay sculptor's tools are a good investment. Otherwise, a toothpick, craft knife, metal nail file, or paintbrush make fine alternatives. These tools are used to add texture to a piece, such as drapes or ruffles in a dress, or facial expressions.

The instructions for many of the projects in this book direct you to first cover a base with an initial layer of mache and then add details

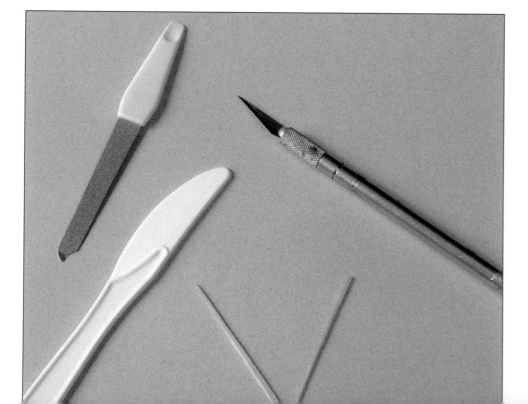

Clay sculpting tools or these handy alternatives are used to add texture and detail to projects.

Molds and Bases for Paper and Fabric Mache

In the good old days, a base for a paper mache project consisted of molded chicken wire. For today's crafters, the possibilities are a bit more intriguing. Begin by searching through your home for interesting containers. Balloons, oatmeal boxes, metal containers, glass bowls, and foam shapes all work well. Molds are used just to support your project's shape while it's wet; they are removed after the fabric or paper dries. Bases, also known as armatures, are not removed, and become an unseen part of the finished project. Another interesting material, plaster wrap (shown above), allows crafters to enlarge a rough-shape base in just a few minutes, instead of spending hours building up the space with layers of paper-mache. To prevent the fabric or paper from sticking, apply a layer of petroleum jelly or aerosol cooking spray.

Fabric box molded over a large plastic container

Left, roll of plaster wrap; assortment of molds and bases

Instant paper-mache is kneaded in a plastic freezer bag to remove lumps and achieve a claylike texture.

A large ball of kneaded mache is rolled into an even thickness.

in additional layers. Because of the glue binder in the mache, layers will adhere without glue by gently pressing them together with dampened fingertips or a dampened paintbrush. Shapes of mache — such as triangles, ovals, and squares — are frequently used to form details such as a nose or cheeks. Although it may seem like a needless step to cut out a precise shape of mache, you'll save yourself a lot of frustration and be rewarded with a nicer finished project if you heed the project designer's advice.

Instant paper-mache is not as messy as the newspaper method, although you'll still need to protect your work area with a layer of plastic wrap. Begin by reading the manufacturer's instructions for mixing the mache. Save a little of the dry mixture in case your mache is too damp and you need to adjust the texture. Mix the mache and the called-for amount of warm water in a plastic freezer bag. Knead the water and pulp together on a flat surface until all the dry spots disappear. Empty the mache mixture out onto the plastic. The texture should be like clay, not too stiff and not too loose. Carefully add a little more water or a little more pulp if the texture needs adjusting. Place another sheet of plastic wrap over the mache and roll it into an even thickness of about 1/4 to 1/2 inch (6 to 13 mm). For children's projects, you can add a few drops of liquid dish detergent to make the mache easier to work with.

After you've finished shaping your project, you will need to pay careful attention to the drying process. If you've used a mold, allow at least 24 hours for the outside layer of mache to dry, and then another 24 hours after you've removed the mold for the inside to dry. For nonmolded projects, such as jewelry beads and cookie cutter ornaments, the ideal drying location is on a cake rack. Turn the mache over once or twice a day to prevent the edges from curling. As the water evaporates from the mache, look for the piece to lighten in color and to become lighter in weight.

Fabric-Mache Techniques

The process of stiffening fabric has been around for a long time. Victorians stiffened lace in a sugar water mixture for a variety of uses. Today, craft stores offer a nice selection of commercially prepared stiffening products, and crafters also have the option of creating homemade mixtures with white craft glue diluted with water. It would be dishonest to mince words here — stiffening fabric is a messy craft. The mess is short-lived and easily cleaned up, though, and for a few glorious minutes while you're applying the stiffening mixture you'll feel like a world-famous painter.

Spread out a layer of aluminum foil or plastic wrap to protect your work surface. (Newspaper becomes a massive mess when exposed to the mache mixture.) Place your fabric with its right side facing down and coat the wrong side with a layer of mache with a paintbrush or your fingers. You should apply enough stiffening medium to saturate the fibers but not so much that it drips off. Alternately, you can dip the entire piece of fabric into the mache mixture, taking care to wring out any excess mache.

Arrange the fabric over your chosen mold with the right side facing outward and apply a layer of mache to the fabric. Form folds, pleats, or gathers in the fabric if desired. Reinforce any areas where the fabric overlaps (folds, pleats, etc.) with additional stiffening mixture. Gently finger-press the fabric in place. If portions of your fabric are not resting against the mold (such as the hat on page 84), you may need to arrange small boxes or towels under the suspended fabric for support during the drying process. (Be sure to place a layer of plastic wrap between the fabric and your supports to prevent adhesion.)

When the fabric has completely dried, you can remove it from the mold. Some molds will slip right out of the fabric, while others will need to be gently coerced the same way you'd encourage a cake to come out of its pan.

Finish any raw edges with the method of your choice: trim them with a utility knife and apply an anti-fray product; fold them under and glue in place; or glue a decorative row of ribbon or lace on top of them.

A word about timing . . .

Stopping in the middle of a project for a few minutes to flip the roast or put in a load of wash won't hurt anything; a conversation with a long-winded phone salesperson could ruin your project. If your fabric dries in a shape you don't care for, place it in the sink and sprinkle it with water until the mache mixture starts to dissolve. Re-mold it into the shape you'd like, and apply additional mache mixture.

Fabrics

Fabrics should be washed before macheing to ensure that any shrinkage will happen before you begin. Especially stubborn wrinkles may refuse to leave even after the fabric's been soaked in mache mixture, so you

Making Stiffened Bows

Yes, a simple stiffened bow can be made without all the steps described below. Just dip a strip of fabric in stiffener and tie it into a bow. But if you want a large double bow with a designer look, it pays to follow these steps developed by master bow maker, Avis Everett. Although the most popular use for these bows is on baskets, they can also be used to decorate curtains, tabletops, bedposts, and more.

First, cut out your fabric (you'll need about 1-1/2 yards, 1.4 m) according to the cutting diagram below. Place the 54-inch streamer on a work-protected surface with its right side facing up. Pour a small amount of stiffening medium on the center of the fabric, and spread it evenly down the fabric with your fingers. Turn the strip over and repeat the process on the other side.

Fold both sides of the fabric strip lengthwise into the center, allowing for a slight overlap. Press deep creases into the folded areas, squeezing out any excess stiffening medium and any wrinkles or air pockets as you work. Lift the strip by one end, secure it to a clothes hanger with a clothespin, and allow it to dry. Now repeat the above steps with all the remaining strips. When the strips have dried enough to be crispy on the edges but are still slightly wet on the outside (approximately 45 minutes, but the time can vary depending on the type of fabric and humidity), you are ready to begin forming the bow.

To begin shaping the fabric, cut off the selvage end of the ribbon and mark the center. Use your fingers to gather across the width of the strip, starting on one edge and squeezing the strip from one side to the other until you like the look of the gathers. Hold the gathers in place with a large hair clamp or clothespin, and put this strip aside. Note: For bows that will be displayed off-center, you may want to make one streamer longer than the other.

Working with the longer loop strip with the seam side face up, bring the two ends up to the center, allowing them to overlap about 1.5 inches (4 cm). Squeeze and gather the center of the folded strip with your fingers, starting at one edge and working over to the other. With the fingers of one hand tightly over the center gathers and the overlapped ends, open up the bow's loops with your other hand. Check to be sure the loops are of equal size. Now hold the bow's center loop pieces with a large plastic clothespin while forming more loops. Place this set of loops gently aside while you work with the shorter strip. Now form the second set of loops with

Cut 1 streamer strip 36 inches long x 18 inches wide

Cut 1 streamer strip 32 inches long x 18 inches wide

Cut 1 connector strip 10 inches long x 4 inches wide

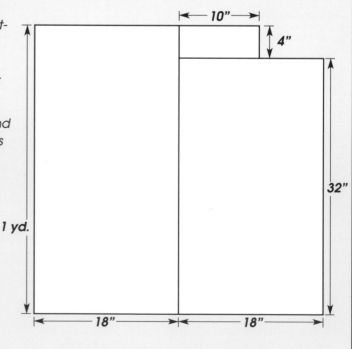

this same technique from the shorter loop strip and set it aside.

Assemble the bow by stacking the larger looped piece on top of the streamer strip, then pinching the layers together. Place the smaller looped piece in place on top of the larger one, then press and pinch all three layers together. Now add a little stiffening medium to the back side of the connector strip. Wrap the strip tightly around all three pieces, allowing the ends to overlap each other on the back side. Trim off any excess length.

Squeeze the connector strip for a minute in the center of the bow to ensure that all three layers will adhere. If the fabric is uncooperative, you can secure the layers together with a little hot glue. To help maintain the shape of your bow loops while the fabric dries, gently stuff them with plastic drinking cups. Create folds in the streamers at this time, and place the bow aside to dry. Note: If you plan to ship a bow project to someone special, it's a good idea to re-stuff the bow loops with cups so they won't be crushed.

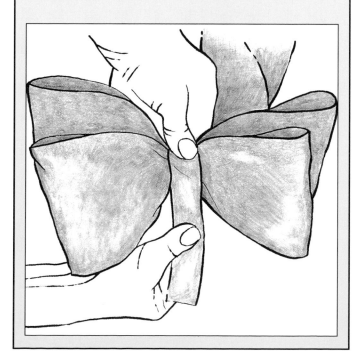

may want to iron the fabric before beginning. Following is a description of how several popular fabrics respond to stiffening.

Cotton fabrics hold their shapes very well, and are probably the best choice for beginning fabric machers. Cotton upholstery fabrics hold their shapes especially well.

Polyester fabrics, especially noncotton blends, do not hold their shapes as well as other types of fabric. Avoid using them unless you're in love with a certain print that you just can't find in cotton and unless you're willing to spend extra time experimenting to find the right mold and the right amount of mache.

Knits mache very well, but the edges of even the 100% cotton varieties roll up, making them a bad choice for fabric-mache projects.

Acetates mache fine, but the fabric is so thin that it's difficult to press out excess mache mixture, making the dried fabric difficult to remove from the mold.

Chintzes are heat-set to hold their colors, so they're easy to cut and the edges won't fray. They are strongly recommended for stiffened bow projects.

Tulle stiffens well, but there's no way to prevent the mache mixture from drying in the open areas of the netting, which is not very attractive.

Cotton burlap holds shapes very well and won't unravel if you're careful to saturate the raw edges with an even coating of mache mixture.

Washable silks will hold a molded shape, but, like acetates, they're so thin that there's no way to remove excess mache mixture, making it extremely difficult to remove them from the mold. Stiffened silk loses its characteristic "silky" look, but the dried fabric is thin enough to allow light to come through — an attractive effect.

Denim fabrics hold their shapes very well, although they're so heavy that they may require extra coatings of mache mixture and props to keep the wet fabric in shape until it dries.

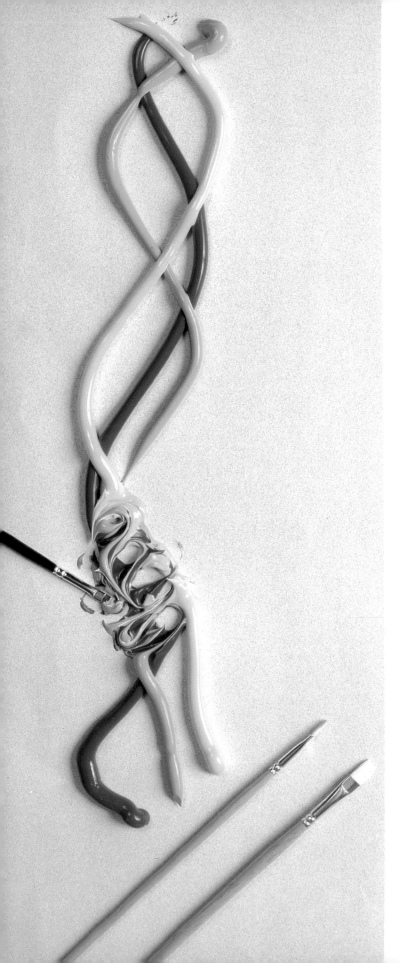

Surface Design

Almost all of the projects in this book were finished with some sort of surface design technique, primarily painting. But even if you've never been happy with anything you've painted, you shouldn't feel intimidated. If you're not happy with your paint job, remove the paint with sandpaper and try again.

It's a good idea to prime the paper-mache surface before painting. Acrylic gesso is the most common product for this purpose. You can find it in the paint department of most craft stores, usually in a selection of several neutral colors. You should never apply gesso to a mache piece that's not completely dry, and you should wait until the gesso is completely dry (12 to 24 hours) before adding paint.

Most mache crafters chose acrylic paints because of their quick drying times and the wide variety of available colors. Choose a paintbrush that's the appropriate size for the area you're working on (i.e., you'd never want to paint facial details with a 1-inch, 2.5 cm, brush). The mache's rough surface causes extensive wear on brushes, so high-quality, expensive brushes are not a good choice. Because the mache's surface area is inherently uneven, the paint may tend to puddle in some areas, so you'll need to be especially careful to allow ample drying time (12 to 24 hours).

After the acrylics dry, apply a layer of clear aerosol sealant. Many of the projects call for you to apply a water-based antiquing medium after the sealant dries. Although it's not absolutely necessary, the antiquing process tends to bring out extra detail and highlights in a project. For very white areas, such as a Santa Claus beard, you may wish to apply a coat of pearl glaze over the antiquing medium (after it dries, of course) to maintain a bright color. After the antiquing medium dries (12 to 24 hours), the piece is finished with another coat of clear aerosol sealant.

Techniques

Other ways to add detail to a project include the dry brushing technique and dimensional fabric paints. To add detail with the dry brushing technique, apply just a little paint to a dry brush and then wipe it on a paper towel, leaving just a hint of color on the brush, and lightly stroke the brush over the piece.

Another way to add color to both paper- and fabric-mache projects is to stir acrylic or water-color paints into the mache mixture before molding. For children's and holiday projects, a layer of glitter can be sprinkled over the mache while it's still wet.

If you plan to display your finished pieces outdoors, you'll need to waterproof them after following the painting steps above with two coats of thin varnish followed by a coat of waterproofing medium from a paint store. Remember to allow each coat to completely dry before adding the next.

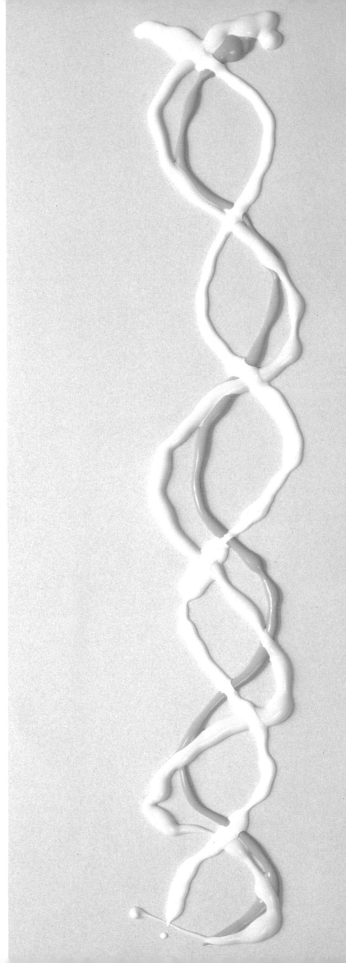

Sunflower Tiles

Painter Diane Weaver devised a clever way to create the look of hand-painted tiles with hardware cloth and instant paper-mache. First cut out a base from exterior plywood and then cover it with a layer of mache about 1/2 inch (12 mm) thick. Next, cover the mache with a tight layer of plastic wrap, overlapping the wrap at the edges and behind the base.

To create an even surface, secure one 1- x 36-inch (2.5 x 92 cm) wooden dowel on each side of the base with tape. Use a third dowel like a rolling pin to form a flat, even surface. Remove the plastic wrap and place a sheet of 1/2-inch grid hardware cloth on top of the mache. Press the cloth into the mache until it's deep enough to create tile-like impressions, but not deep enough to submerge the wire. Carefully remove the hardware cloth after two hours.

After the mache dries (average time: one week), prime the mache with a layer of black gesso and paint the tiles with acrylic paints according to the guide below. To create your own designs, use a color copier to enlarge or reduce a favorite picture to the size you'd like

your finished tile project to be. Then use a dark ink pen to mark off the photo in squares the same size as your hardware

cloth. Note: A smaller or larger size grid of hardware cloth may work better if you choose to do a smaller or larger photo. ❖

Picnic Basket

Adding contrasting colors of paint before she decorates a basket with stiffened fabric motifs and bows is one of interior designer Avis Everett's favorite ways to create a professional-looking craft project. Avis frequently chooses designer curtain fabrics for her projects because she loves the way these cotton chintz fabrics hold their shapes. (See pages 13 and 14 for complete instructions for tying stiffened bows and applying fabric motifs.) ❖

Bulb Vase

Multi-media floral designer Fred Gaylor made these flower containers by macheing silk leaves and brown wrapping paper. To form the vase that resembles a sprouting flower bulb, dip long silk leaves into fabric stiffener and arrange them so they protrude over the top of the vase by about 2 inches (5 cm). Then cut brown construction paper into 1/4- x 4-inch (6 mm x 10 cm) strips and cut their ends into points. Brush the back side of the paper strips with tacky glue and arrange them around the bottom of the vase, folding and gluing the bottom of the strips under the bottom of the base.

For the planter, spray a light layer of green paint around the top of a terra cotta pot. Then soak large silk leaves in fabric stiffener and press them against the pot until they are smooth and arranged in a pleasant pattern. After the leaves dry, finish the pot with a natural raffia bow. ❖

19

Lace Hearts

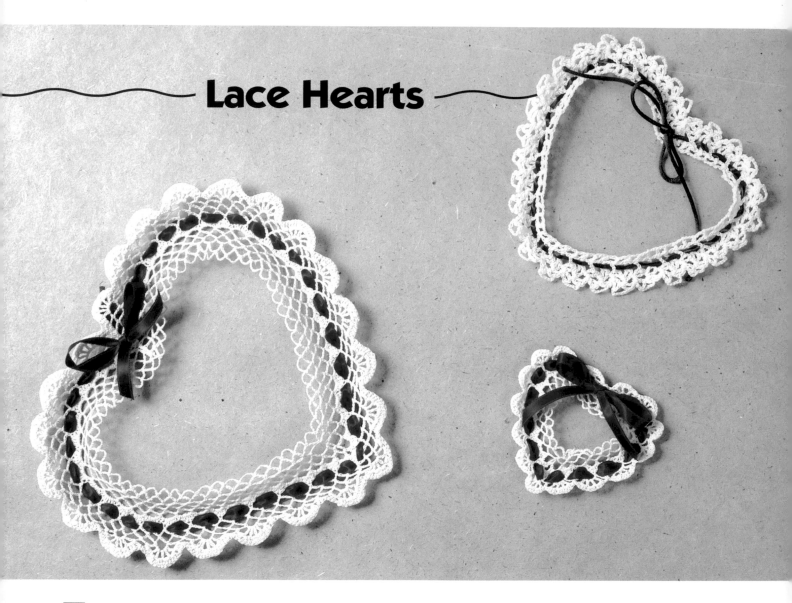

In search of a fabric mache mold that would create a three-dimensional form, Marie-Helene Grabman stumbled upon the idea of creating molds from aluminum foil by shaping a 4-inch (10 cm) wide strip of foil into a heart shape, and then forming a raised ridge in the center. (See illustration.)

After making the molds, loosely arrange several pieces of lace around the form to determine the length and width of lace edging that will look best. Then stitch the two ends of the lace with their right sides together in the narrowest seam allowance possible. Turn the lace right sides out and soak it in fabric stiffener. Remove the excess stiffener from the lace and shape it around the mold. After the lace dries, decorate it with ribbon. Silk or dried flowers can also be used if further embellishment is desired. The small hearts make lovely tree ornaments and package decorations for special gifts, while the larger hearts look nice hanging in a window. ❖

Stiffened Cutwork

Professional papercutter Marie-Helene Grabman enjoyed trying to adapt some of her papercutting techniques to fabric. After much experimenting, Marie-Helene found that most fabrics just weren't stiff enough unless they were reinforced with a layer of iron-on interfacing. Marie adapted the floral pattern from the stiffened fabric motifs on the coordinating basket.

To begin, transfer a flower pattern to the wrong side of a tablecloth, spacing it evenly along the length of the cloth. Stiffen the fabric by ironing on a strip of fusible interfacing to the wrong side. Next, carefully cut out the design with a small pair of sharp embroidery scissors. Stretch the fabric right side facing up over a piece of foil-covered cardboard. Secure the fabric to the cardboard with clothespins or hair clips. Then decorate the edges of the cutouts with fabric paint. ❖

Decoupage Bowl

Designer Mary Beth Ruby recommends this project as an ideal one for beginners because it gives crafters such a good feel for working with instant paper-mache.

To begin, choose a bowl whose shape you're enamored with and cover it with plastic wrap, taping the wrap in place if necessary. After mixing and rolling the mache as directed on page 10, lay the mache around the bowl and smooth the surface with dampened fingertips. Trim the edges with a butter knife for a smooth surface. Leave the bowl in a warm place to dry for at least 24 hours, then pop it off the mold. Allow at least another 24 hours for the inside of the bowl to dry, and then seal the inner and outer surfaces with a layer of acrylic gesso. After the gesso dries, paint the entire bowl with acrylics.

To decoupage the outside of the bowl, coat a small area inside the bowl with acrylic gesso with a wide-bristled brush. Next, use the brush to pick up small pieces of torn tissue paper and lay them onto the wet area. Smooth each piece of tissue against the bowl with the brush, and continue working with this technique until the entire inside of the bowl is covered. ❖

Corner Basket

When crafter Avis Everett gives classes on how to make stiffened bows, she's often amazed that people assume the process is complex. Although this project requires a little time and thought to create a finished appearance, the techniques are quite simple. Avis likes to decorate both the inside and outside of her larger baskets so they can be used to hold magazines or just placed in a corner to look pretty. If you're shipping the basket off to a special friend, Avis recommends placing plastic drinking cups inside the bow loops to prevent them from being crushed. (See pages 13 and 14 for complete instructions on making stiffened bows.) ❖

Whimsical Clock

Multi-media artist Diane Weaver drew inspiration for this whimsical clock from her childhood memories of her energetic mother. To form the base, cut out a 20- x 20-inch (50 x 50 cm) sheet of 3/4-inch (20 mm) thick foam. (See illustration.) Then assemble the main body of the box with white craft glue and T-pins. Cut a hole in the back of the clock large enough to insert the clock works and battery.

Cut out two L-shaped legs from 1/4-inch (6 mm) foam and secure them in place with glue and T-pins. Cover the box form with a 1/8-inch (3 mm) layer of instant paper-mache mixed with a little plaster to add strength. After this layer of mache dries, trace a circle in the center front of the clock from the bottom of a drinking glass. Then roll out coils of mache and place them around the clock face, working in small sections at time and pressing them together. Then press the coils flat and use a pencil to poke in decorative holes.

Cover the legs with a layer of mache and mold the feet with additional mache to form shoes. Next, roll short coils of mache and scallop them 1/2 inch up from the bottom to form the ruffle; then attach a

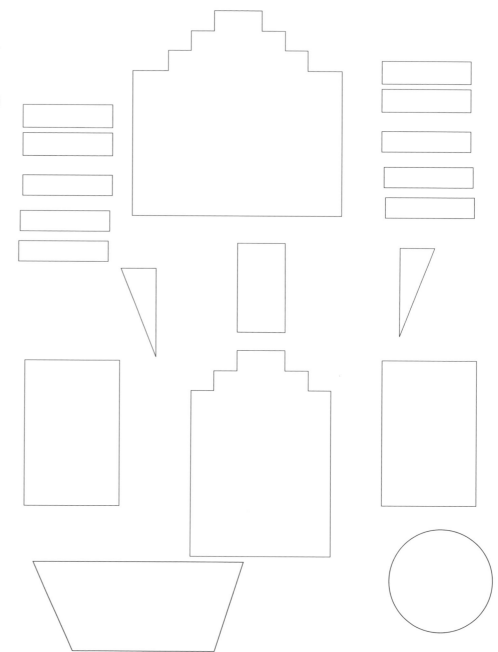

second coil above the first to form a cord over the ruffle. For the face, form an egg-shaped oval of mache for the head and pinch out a nose. Then create small holes for the eye sockets and add small balls of mache for the eyes. Open the mouth with a pencil point.

After the mache in the head area dries, press on a little mache for the hair. Attach a coil for ribbon and a ball for the flower, and use a pencil point to open the flower petals. Next, form the ears with small balls of mache and press them in place. After these new layers of mache dry, roll out two coils of mache and place them on top of each other to form the neck. To attach the head to the clock base, press a 3-inch (7.5 cm) nail 1 inch into the head, and then gently push the nail though the center of the neck until the head makes firm contact.

To form the hands, mold mache over a paper clip that has been opened up on one end. After the mache dries, press the protruding end of the paper clip into the foam. To prevent the paint from absorbing down into the mache, apply a coat of acrylic gesso. After the gesso dries, apply color with acrylic paints with a variety of different sized brushes. When the paint dries, finish with a light layer of clear acrylic spray. ❖

Designer Marie-Helene Grabman decorated a wicker basket and tray with stiffened fabric motifs to create the perfect combination for summer entertaining. To begin, spray paint an inexpensive wicker basket and tray in a color that will contrast well with your fabric's motifs. Paint the details in the basket and tray with gloss enamel paint in a contrasting color to add style.

After the paint dries, carefully cut out the fabric motifs with sharp scissors so that none of the background colors show. (Note: Chintz or polished cotton make good fabric choices for these projects.) Apply a layer of fabric adhesive (sold commercially under several different brand names) to the backs of the motifs and then press them flat against the wicker surfaces with a warm, damp cloth. After the fabric dries, apply another layer of fabric adhesive to the top of the motifs with a paint brush. When the motifs dry for the second time, spray the entire basket with a layer of clear glaze. ❖

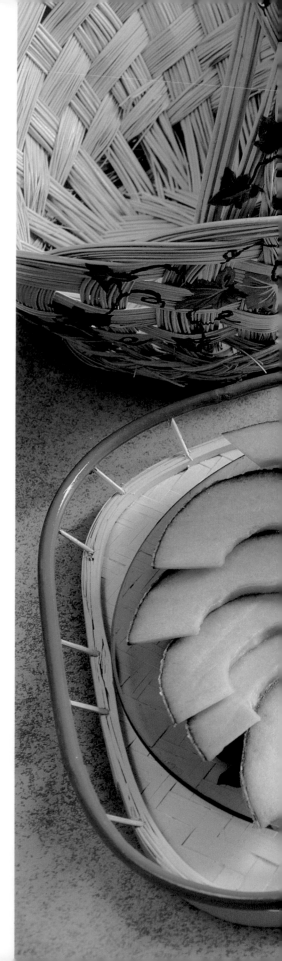

Fruit Bowl

This bowl represents Anne McCloskey's first attempt to work with instant paper-mache, and she says it will probably be her last. Anne simply prefers watching the shape and thickness of a project evolve with the steady slowness that comes from applying newspaper strips one layer at a time.

For this bowl, turn a large glass bowl upside down and cover the outside with a protective layer of petroleum jelly. Apply six or seven layers of mache around the bowl, taking care to keep the thickness of the mache mixture relatively consistent over the entire bowl. After the mache completely dries (several days), carefully lift

it from around the edges of the bowl and remove it. Allow the bowl another few days to finish drying, and then paint on a layer of gesso. When the gesso dries, apply dabs of pastel colors with a wide brush. ❖

Sunflower Delights

Since Diane Weaver and husband Dick spend much of their time in the display gardens that are part of their business, Gourmet Gardens, Diane decided to add some year 'round color with these mache sunflowers.

To form a base for the larger flower, cut petal shapes into a plastic lid from a coffee or oatmeal canister. Gently hold the lid over a heat source until the petals begin to fold up and curl. Cover with instant papermache and press a metal rod or a thick natural stem into the mache on the back side. Pinch the center circle of the flower in an allover pattern to form seed-like shapes. Allow to completely dry, then seal with gesso, paint, and waterproof according to the basic instructions of page 15.

Sunflowers can also be made from solid mache, like the smaller flower. First form a large cookie shape of mache, using a paper plate as a pattern. Push a pencil about halfway through the back side of the cookie and then remove it to form a hole for the stem. Allow the mache to dry until damp, and then form egg-size oval of mache for the petals. Press each shape of mache in place. Place your thumb and index finger on the top side of the petals and the rest of your fingers underneath, then gently squeeze at the tip to form interesting petal shapes. Pinch the center circle of the flower in an allover pattern to form seed-like shapes. Glue in a metal rod or thick natural stem, then finish as directed for flower above. ❖

Mache Candelabra

Ever-imaginative designer Diane Weaver encourages crafters not to be intimidated by the directions for this project. A trip to the local hardware store should yield all the materials you'll need. First cut a 44-inch length (110 cm) of 12- x 3/8-inch (30 cm x 10 mm) copper plumbing tubing and form it in a circle around a 14-inch (36 cm) dish. Tap the ends with a tack hammer until the circle is well formed. Cut the tubing circle in half with a hack saw. Make a second 14-inch circle, then an 11-inch circle, and then cut both circles in half.

Mark the center of each of the half circles and use pliers to flatten the tubes on both sides of the center marks so that you have 1 inch of flat space at the center of each arch. (See illustration.) Then use an awl to make an indentation at the center of the center mark on all of the half-circles, and drill a 1/4-inch (6 mm) hole at the center points.

Next, form a tube circle around a 5-inch plate and overlap the ends by 1.5 inches (4 cm). Flatten 1 inch of each end of this circle and make another flat space at a point half the circumference. Pierce the center of the flattened area as you did the other pieces and drill a 1/4-inch hole. Cut a length of

3-foot x 1/3-inch (2.7 m x 9 mm) rod to 24 inches (60 cm). Starting with the center circle, begin assembling the candelabra with 1/4-inch nuts and tubes. (Do not tighten the nuts until you have everything in order.) Check the spaces on the top arches by measuring the space between tube ends.

Wrap the entire armature with a layer of plaster-impregnated wrap. Leave 1/4 inch bare at the top of the tube that the candle holder will slide over. When the wrap dries, measure the distance from the center rod below the circle, pierce the tube at that spot, and screw in two or three sheet metal screws. Cut a 2-foot x 1/8-inch (1.8 m x 3 mm) rod to fit, cutting the ends at an angle so they will fit snug and upright against the legs.

Cover the armature with a second layer of plaster wrap to cover the joints where the 1/8-inch rod meets the main armature and over the screw connection. After the plaster wrap dries, cover the armature with instant paper-mache, forming shapes on the main rod by squeezing your hands, spreading your fingers, and then smoothing. Attach other shapes to the candle arch bottoms by forming pea-sized ovals of mache and smoothing them in place, then form the feet.

Form the center holding dish by molding mache over the item you plan to display there. After

the mache dries, remove the ball and then attach it to the end of the threaded rod using a small ball of mache and hot glue. Position the candle holders on the bare 1/4-inch tube

ends and level them. Fill them halfway with hot glue and hold them in place for a minute or two until the glue cools. Finish by spraying the entire candelabra black with acrylic paint. ❖

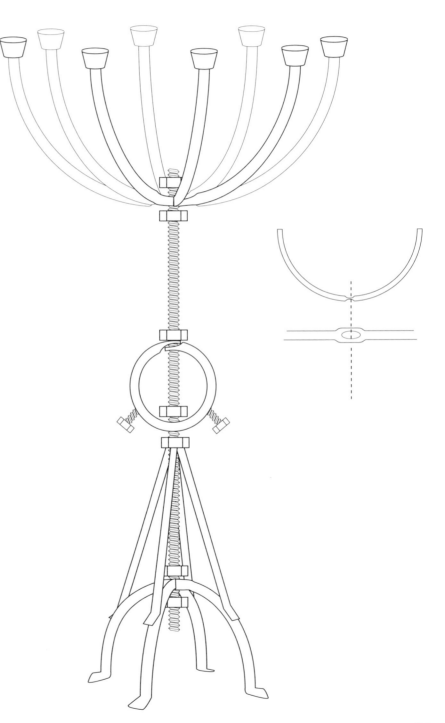

Sewing Basket

Designer Anne McCloskey, who frequently takes a playful approach to her craft designs, created this sewing basket with both stiffened paper and fabric.

First prepare the mold by covering the inside of a large bowl with a thin layer of petroleum jelly. Then cut several sheets of heavy construction paper into small squares and coat them in white craft glue that's been diluted with water. Position the squares over the outside of the bowl, overlapping them until you have five or six layers.

Once the paper squares dry, remove the bowl from the mold and allow it to finish drying. Coat squares of calico fabric with the glue mixture and arrange them around the inside of the bowl. To finish, glue small silk flowers on top of the fabric and paper squares around the bowl. ❖

Dining Tray

Avis Everett's first craft project was stenciling her historic Atlanta-area home in the traditional patterns that once adorned it, and Avis' love of stenciling is evident in most of her stiffened fabric projects.

To create the painted wicker look, attach ivy and pansy fabric cutouts, stiffen and form the bows as directed on pages 13 and 14, and hot-glue them to the tray after they've dried. ❖

Candle Vase

Designer Fred Gaylor has always had a passion for decorating with candles and lights, and he enjoys the design versatility of fabric mache. To create this customized candle holder, cut a large circle of fabric, dip it in fabric stiffener, and then fold the fabric around a tall vase. Press out any excess stiffener, and tie the vase with leather shoe laces. ❖

An experimental crafter at heart, Doris Neisler's first attempts with fabric mache yielded these decorative table projects. To create the napkin rings, she cotes both sides of a 3- x 7-inch (7.5 to 17 cm) strip of fabric with stiffener and then fold it in thirds lengthwise. Shape the fabric around an empty paper towel roll that's been covered with plastic wrap. After the rings completely dry, wrap a short length of pipe cleaner around the area where the two ends meet. Thread the beads over the pipe cleaner and finish by hot-gluing a small feather into one of the end beads.

To create the fabric basket, trace and cut out a circle shape from a dinner plate from two pieces of fabric and one piece of fusible webbing. Following the manufacturer's instructions, use the webbing to fuse the two pieces of fabric together, with their wrong sides facing. Form the handle from a 3- x 8-inch (7.5 to 20 cm) strip of fabric, folding and stiffening it as you did the with the napkin rings. Coat both sides of the fabric circles with stiffening agent. Mold the handle and the circles around an oatmeal box that has been covered in plastic wrap, and allow it to dry overnight. Remove the forms, position the handle over the

Fabric Basket & Napkin Rings

bowl. Make holes where the basket and the handle overlap on both sides with a hole puncher. Secure the handle to the basket with a piece of pipe cleaner in a contrasting color, and thread the beads onto the pipe cleaner. Finish by hot-gluing some small feathers into the end of the beads. ❖

Holiday Basket

Avis Everett created this decorative table centerpiece from a plain, inexpensive basket and a few scraps of holiday fabric. When choosing a fabric for her projects, Avis looks for patterns that aren't too cluttered and with a distinct color difference between the design and the background. During the busy holiday season, Avis carries fabric scraps and sharp scissors with her so she can spend every bit of time productively and have lovely gifts to share with her friends. ❖

Victorian Boxes

Designer Nicole Victoria enjoys creating lavish Victorian-styled containers from plain cardboard boxes. First measure the surface areas of the boxes, and cut out the fabric to fit. Saturate the fabric with stiffener and position it against the boxes, pressing out any air bubbles and excess stiffener with your fingers. After the fabric completely dries, use a glue gun to add gathers of lace, silk flowers, and ribbon, positioning some of them to cover areas where fabric sections meet. ❖

Pencil Holder

Designer Sarah Kim used an empty jelly jar as the base for this pencil holder. First cover the jar with a layer of instant paper-mache, and then use a butter knife to create a zigzag pattern in the mache. After the mache completely dries, prime it with a layer of acrylic gesso and then paint it with a fun assortment of primary acrylic colors. ❖

Flower Vase

Wearable fiber artist Anne McCloskey enjoys spending her free time on just about any type of craft. To create the vessel shown here, first coat the outside of a vase with petroleum jelly. Then apply five layers of newspaper strips that have been coated in a mache mixture. After the mache had dries, remove the vase and allow the inside to finish drying.

Paint the entire surface with a layer of gesso to prevent the newsprint from showing through. When the gesso dries, begin painting dark blue flowers onto the vase. (Use a floral wallpaper or gift wrap as a guide for floral shapes if you doubt your artistic talent.) Next, paint over and around some of the flowers with white paint to achieve varying shades of

blue. After the paint dries, apply a layer of gloss (call her and find out what type of gloss) and then paint the inside of the vase with gesso. If you choose to use the vessel as a vase for fresh flowers, you can prevent water leakage by arranging them in a bottle or jar slightly smaller than the vase and then slipping the bottle down into the vase. ❖

Doggie Bed

Fred Gaylor made this dog bed for Pepper, the special canine in his life. Fred used fabric left over from a recent decorating binge, so the bed matches his bedspread and curtains.

First paint a wicker basket with enamel paint. While the paint dries, cut down a piece of foam to fit inside the basket and cover the foam with fabric, using hot glue to secure it on the back side. ❖

Terra Cotta Planter

Although most of her finished work is displayed sitting flat, Mary Beth Ruby has always enjoyed wall hangings, so working out the kinks in this project was a labor of love. First roll out a large rectangle of mache. Trim the edges with a sharp knife to form rounded corners, and make a hole in the center for hanging. Check to make sure the edges are not thinner than the center of the sheet. (If the edges are thinner, they will tend to curl as they dry.)

After the mache completely dries, roll out another sheet of mache about one-third as long and 2 inches (5 cm) wider than the first sheet. Coat a small bowl whose width and depth will fit on the bottom half of the dried mache with petroleum jelly, and then position it on the right side of the rectangle near the bottom. Mold the wet sheet of mache against the sides and bottom of the bowl, sealing the edges well with dampened fingers.

After the mache pocket is about half-way dry, slide the bowl out and allow it to finish drying. Fill any cracks that have appeared during the drying process with wet mache, smoothing well with wet fingers. Decorate the outside of the pocket with small shapes (berries, flowers, leaves, etc.) that you've cut out with a sharp knife from a sheet of rolled-out mache. Press the shapes onto the pocket surface, making sure they're well attached, and then allow them to dry. When the piece is completely dry, seal it with a coat of gesso. Then paint with acrylics, and finish with a coat of clear varnish, allowing each coat to completely dry before adding the next. ❖

FIGURES AND FORMS

Summer Strolls

An antique paper-mache figurine served as Dolly Lutz Morris' original inspiration for these pieces, and these pieces, in turn, have inspired several new generations of figurines. Dolly chose to do a lamb for her other piece because she, like the Victorians, enjoys personifying animals with human expressions and deeds.

Lady Margaret Elizabeth Cat

Form a cone base from poster board that's 9 inches (22 cm) high with a base that's 3 inches (7.5 cm) in diameter. Next, tape the middle of a 9-inch length of medium-gauge floral wire to the cone 1/2 inch (12 mm) from the top to form a base for the arms and shoulders. Do not bend the wire yet. Cover the cone with a 1/4- to 1/2 inch (6 to 12 mm) layer of instant-paper mache, covering the wire at the shoulder area only, and then add a 1-inch (2.5 cm) ball of mache at the top of the cone to form the head's rough shape. Allow the mache to completely dry before continuing.

Add two smaller balls of mache to the head to form the cat's cheeks, one small ball for the nose and mouth area, and two small balls that have been shaped into inverted Vs for the ears. Use a metal nail file to sculpt and shape the features. Next, bend the arm wires into the desired positions and cover them with mache to form the arms and paws. Shape a small coil of mache into a foot and press it in place at the bottom of the cone. Allow all of the mache to completely dry before continuing. Then seal the piece with gesso, paint, apply a coat of aerosol sealant, antique, and finish with another coat of sealant, allowing each coat to completely dry before adding the next. (See complete instructions for these steps on page 15.)

Next cut an 18- x 7-inch (46 x 17 cm) rectangle of satin fabric and sew the short sides together to form a tube. Sew a strip of lace to the bottom and sew a row of gathering stitches at the top. Dip the fabric into stiffener and pull the tube up from the cone's bottom to the waist area. Pull the gathers tight at the waist, knot the thread, and arrange gathers in the skirt.

While the skirt is drying, cut a circle from poster board that's

2.5 inches (6.5 cm) in diameter with a 1.25-inch (3 cm) hole cut out from the center. Cut out a 7-inch fabric circle and dip it in stiffener. Arrange the fabric over the brim with the crown of the hat puffed up. Drape the fabric under the brim and inside the crown and allow to dry. Then add ribbon and beads for decoration and glue the hat to the cat's head. Now glue ribbon cuffs above the paws, lace and pearls around the neck, and the shawl (a crocheted doily) around the shoulders and under the paw.

Mother Rabbit

Form a base for the body and the arms from poster board and wire as you did for Lady Margaret Elizabeth Cat. For the ears, bend a 12-inch (30 cm) length of medium-gauge floral wire into an M shape, tape the bottom together, and tape it to the back of the cone's top. Now cover the cone with a 1/4- to 1/2-inch layer of mache, covering the wire at the shoulder area only. Add a 1-inch ball of mache at the top of the cone where the cone meets the ear wires to form the head's rough shape. Allow the mache to completely dry before continuing.

Cover the ear wires with a layer of mache and indent the center of the ear with a metal nail file. Next add small balls of mache to the head to form the nose and cheeks as you did with Margaret Elizabeth. Bend the arm wires into the desired

positions and cover them with mache to form the arms and paws. Shape a small coil of mache into a foot and press it in place at the bottom of the cone. Allow all of the mache to completely dry before continuing.

For the baby rabbit's body, place a 1-inch ball of mache into the bent arm for the body. Insert an 8-inch (20 cm) length of floral wire that's been bent into an M shape into the body for the ear base, and add a 1/2-inch ball of mache for the head. Cover the ear wires with mache. Form the baby's arm from a 1-inch cylinder of mache, attach it to the body, and shape as needed. After the mache completely dries, seal the piece with gesso, paint, apply a coat of aerosol sealant, antique, and finish with another coat of sealant, allowing each coat to completely dry before adding the next.

For the skirt, sew the short sides of a plaid fabric rectangle measuring 12 x 7 inches (30 x 17 cm) to form a tube. Turn under the bottom edge and sew a row of gathering stitches. Dip the fabric in stiffener and pull the tube up over the cone from the bottom. Pull the gathers tight, knot off the thread, and arrange drapes in the skirt.

While the mother rabbit's skirt is drying, form a skirt for the baby by sewing the short sides of a 3- x 6-inch (7.5 x 15 cm) rectangle of lace together. Sew a

row of gathering stitches, pull them tight, and dip the tube in fabric stiffener. After the skirt has dried, glue it to the mother's skirt under her arm. To finish, glue a length of stiffened lace around the mother and baby's faces to form the brim of their bonnets. Glue bows under their chins, and glue a basket of dried flowers in Mother Rabbit's hand.

Mrs. Lamb

Form a base for the body and arms as you did for Lady Elizabeth Margaret Cat. Cover the cone with a 1/4- to 1/2-inch layer of mache, covering the wire at the shoulder area only. Add a 1-inch ball of mache at the top of the cone, where it meets the ear wires, to form the head's rough shape. Allow the mache to completely dry before continuing.

To form the face features, add two small balls of mache for the cheeks and long nose, and indent the mouth shape with a metal nail file. Add a 1-inch ball at the back to form the puffy shape of the bonnet's back. Add a little mache around the face and indent it with the file to create the look of textured fur. For the ears, shape two 1-inch lengths of wire into V shapes and insert them into the wet mache. After the mache completely dries, cover each ear with mache and indent the center of the ears with the nail file.

Bend the arm wires into the

desired position and cover them with mache, forming the paws as you work. After the mache completely dries, seal the piece with gesso, paint, apply a coat of aerosol sealant, antique, and finish with another coat of sealant, allowing each coat to completely dry before adding the next.

Form the skirt from a calico print as you did for Mother Rabbit, and glue a length of stiffened lace around the face to form the bonnet's brim. Glue a bow under the chin, and glue a shawl (a crocheted doily) around her shoulders and under the paw. Last, glue a small basket of dried flowers to the extended paw. ❖

Marital Bliss

These bridal bunnies were a commissioned project for dollmaker Dolly Lutz Morris. The client wanted the bunnies designed as a wedding gift, with the bride bunny's bouquet matching the real-life bride and the groom bunny holding a book inscribed with the bridal couple's names. The expressions on the rabbits' faces are reminiscent of the Victorian period, when animal figurines were personified with human expressions.

Make the base for Sweet Bunny, one of the wedding guests, from a cone of poster board secured with tape, measuring 5 inches tall and 2.5 inches (12 x 6.5 cm) at the base. Form the arms by bending a 6-inch (15 cm) length of medium-gauge floral wire into an M shape and taping the bottoms together. (See illustration.) Tape the wire shape to the top of the cone to form a base for the ears. Make a pencil mark 4 inches (10 cm) up from the base and cover this area with a 1/2-inch (13 mm) layer of instant-paper mache. With a metal nail file, press in skirt ruffles and allow the mache to completely dry before continuing.

Next, add a 1-inch (2.5 cm) ball of mache above the shoulder area (2.75 inches, 8 cm up from the base) for a head. Add two small balls of mache for the cheeks, blending them in place, and press in nose and mouth impressions with the nail file. For the arms, roll out two 3-inch (7.5 cm) coils of mache, bend them at the elbow area, and press them in place. Use the nail file to form indents where the sleeves and paws meet, and allow the arms to completely dry before continuing.

Prime, paint, seal, antique, and seal again, allowing each layer to completely dry before adding the next. When the final coat of sealant dries, glue strips of gathered lace around the bottom of the skirt and around the head to form the bonnet rim. Last, glue a bow of narrow satin ribbon under the chin.

Basket Bunny

Place a 1.5-inch (4 cm) ball of mache inside a small basket for the rabbit's body. (The top should protrude slightly above the basket's rim.) Then place a 1-inch ball of mache on top of the body for the head, and blend the two balls together at the neck. Next, add two small balls of mache to the head to form cheeks. Indent the nose and mouth with the pointed end of a metal nail file. For the ears, bend a 5-inch (12 cm) length of medium-gauge floral wire into an M shape. Twist the bottom of the wire together

and insert it into the top of the head. Allow the mache to completely dry before continuing.

Roll out a 1.5-inch coil of mache for the arm and paw. Press it against the side of the body, draping the paw over the basket and slightly flattening the coil as you work. After the arm completely dries, seal with gesso, paint, seal, antique, and seal again, allowing each coat to completely dry before adding the next. (See complete instructions for these steps on page 15.) When the last coat dries, glue lace around the rabbit's face for the bonnet brim and glue a ribbon bow under the chin. Finish by decorating the inside of the basket and the rim with Spanish moss and small dried flowers.

Bridal Bunnies

Begin by making the bunnies' bench from a rectangle of mache measuring 2 x 4.5 inches (5 x 11.5 cm) and 1/4 inch (6 mm) thick. Insert a twig measuring 1.75 inches long x 1/4 inch in diameter (41 x 6 mm) in each of the four corners for bench legs. Allow the bench to completely dry before continuing. Next make a base from a rectangle of mache measuring 5.5 x 4 inches (13.5 x 10 cm) that's 1/4-inch thick. Insert the bench legs into the mache so that the back of the bench is even with the back of the base and allow to completely dry before continuing.

To begin the bride, form a skirt from a flattened triangle of mache that's 4 inches wide at the base and 3 inches high. Use a metal nail file to press in the drapes of the skirt. Then make a small cardboard cone that's 2.5 inches high and 1.5 inches at the base for the torso. Press the skirt on the bench and cover the cone with a thin layer of mache. Allow the mache to completely dry before continuing.

For the bride's head, press a 1-inch ball of mache on top of the torso and use a nail file to blend it in at the neck. Next, bend a 6-inch length of medium-gauge floral wire into an M shape and twist the ends together at the bottom. Insert the wire into the head to form the base for the ears and cover them with mache. Add two small balls of mache for the cheeks and press in the nose and mouth features with the nail file. For the bride's arms and paws, press a 3-inch coil of mache on each side, creating paw indents and fabric drapes with the nail file. Seal with gesso, paint, add aerosol sealant, antique, and add a final coat of sealant, allowing each coat to completely dry before adding the next. (See complete instructions for these steps on page 15.)

For the groom, form the knees from two poster board cones measuring 2 inches long and 1/2 inch in diameter and position them in place next to the bride. Cover the cones with a layer of mache. Next add small balls of mache at the bottom of each cone and shape them into feet. For the torso, place a poster board cone measuring 3 inches tall and 2 inches in diameter at the base onto the bench and cover it with a layer of mache. Indent the front with the nail file to create a jacket lapel. Then make two coils for the tops of the legs (from knees to torso), blending and shaping them with the nail file. For the arm, press a 4-inch coil of mache that's been bent at the elbow area to the side opposite the bride. Create indents in the mache with the nail file where the paw and sleeve meet. Allow the mache to completely dry before continuing.

Finish the groom's head as you did the bride's. Next, press two triangles of mache under his chin for the bow tie and place a round ball on the bride's shoulder for his other paw. (Her veil will cover the arm.) Allow the mache to completely dry before continuing. Seal with gesso, paint, add aerosol sealant, antique, and finish with another coat of sealant, allowing each coat to completely dry before continuing with the next. (See complete instructions for these steps on page 15.) To finish the piece, glue a length of gathered lace to the bottom of the bride's skirt and glue a 3-inch lace square to her head for the veil. Next, glue craft pearls around the top of the veil and glue ribbon roses in the bride's hands. ❖

Flamingo

This bathing flamingo, appropriately named *Bird Bath* is a popular item with Mary Beth Ruby's customers. Because Mary Beth does not use molds, though, the facial expressions and poses of each flamingo vary with each piece.

To form the tub's base, first widen one of the short ends of a shoe box by making 1-inch-deep cuts in the two corners. For the tub's feet, first make a hole through the box where you'd like the feet to be. Press a length of plastic-coated clothesline wire through one of the holes and then bend it into a foot shape. Reinsert the wire back through the hole and then move to the next foot location. Repeat until you have shaped all four feet, then cut the wire. Turn the box upside down (so the feet are in the air) and cover the feet wires with mache. Allow to completely dry before turning the tub right side up.

Form the outline of the flamingo with another long length of clothesline wire, and then fill out the bird's shape by wrapping strips of newspaper around the wire, taping to secure as needed. Place the flamingo form in the tub with the back of the bird resting against the wide end of the tub, and cover the bird with chunks of foam to hold him in place. Roll out a large rectangle of instant paper-mache as directed on page 10, and piece it over the outside of the box. Roll out another rectangle of mache for the water and position it on top of the foam.

Next, cover the bird with a layer of mache, adding extra mache and shaping as needed. Spend some extra time smoothing the areas where the bird meets the water. Form the faucet fixtures from mache and press them in place. After the mache is completely dry, prime it with gesso, then paint with acrylics, and finish with a coat of clear varnish, allowing each coat to completely dry before adding the next. ❖

Sleepy

This project was inspired by an antique molded ornament owned by designer Dolly Lutz Morris' aunt. Begin the figurine by making a cone armature from poster board measuring 5 inches high by 1.5 inches across (12 x 4 cm) and securely taping it closed. Slide a paper clip down into the top center of the cone, leaving 1/4 inch (6 mm) protruding. Cover the cone with a thin layer of instant paper-mache and allow it to dry.

Make a pencil mark 4 inches (10 cm) up from the bottom of the cone to mark the shoulder area. Apply another layer of mache from this mark down; after this layer dries, apply another layer of mache to the entire cone. Create drapes in the skirt fabric and ruffles at the bottom with the rounded end of a metal nail file. Allow the figure to dry.

Press a 1-inch (2.5 cm) ball of mache over the top of the cone for the head, allowing a little of the paper clip to protrude so the ribbon hanger can be threaded through it. Continue shaping the head and blend it into the shoulder area. Press in a circle where the face and bonnet meet with the pointed end of the nail file. Roll two 1.5-inch coils for the arms and press them in place.

Babe ───

Create indents in the mache for the hands.

After the mache dries, coat the piece with a layer of acrylic gesso. Glue a length of lace around the ruffle of the skirt. Next, paint the doll's gown, bonnet, and lace with antique white acrylic paint, and then paint the rest of the doll. Make a small bow from embroidery floss and glue it under the doll's chin. Tie a bow at the top of the bonnet, stringing it through the paper clip, and then tie both ends together to form a hanger. After the paint dries, spray with sealant, apply a coat of antiquing medium, and finish with another coat of spray sealant, allowing each coat to completely dry before adding the next. ❖

Honey Bear

Dottie Shultz has been collecting teddy bears for years, and she often draws inspiration for her paper-mache projects from a special bear in her collection. First form the base by dipping the tips of two toothpicks into craft glue and then inserting one end of the picks into a 2-inch (5 cm) foam ball and the other ends into a 2.5-inch (6.5 cm) foam ball. Then slice off a small piece of the large foam ball with a serrated knife to create a flat surface for the bear to rest on.

Cover the bear with a layer of instant paper-mache, working the mache with your damp-

ened fingers until the surface area is smooth. To form the ears, roll two pieces of mache into balls about the size of a small lima bean and press each ball around the end of your thumb to form an ear. Press the ears in place on the smaller ball. For the muzzle, roll out a quarter-sized piece of mache into a ball, flatten it into an oval, and press it in place on the small ball.

For the bear's arms, make two tubes, each about 2 inches long, with one end a little thicker than the other. Press the arms in place on the bears's body about two-thirds of the way down, using the thicker end for the shoulder. Use a toothpick to score a thumb at the top of the paws, and then use a dampened brush to finish shaping. For the legs, form two pieces of mache the size of a golf ball into legs with feet. Add the legs to the body, taking care to ensure there will be enough room between the feet to add the candle cup. For the tail, press a marble-sized

ball of mache against the bear's center back, and then use a toothpick to create furlike texture. Seal all of the joining areas with a dampened brush as you work.

Press the candle cup between the feet so it touches the bear's belly. Add some mache to the bottom and work it back into the belly. Move the paws so they rest on the edge of the cup. Check the bear for any fingerprints or rough spots, and make sure the bear is sitting level. Leave the bear on a drying rack until he's completely hardened, then apply a coat of acrylic gesso to seal. After the gesso dries, paint with acrylics, seal with a layer of aerosol spray, antique, and finish with another layer of spray, allowing each coat to completely dry before continuing with the next. Pour some melted beeswax into the candle cup, allowing some of the wax to drip down the sides. For an extra touch, drip a little wax down the bear's mouth and on his arms. ❖

Dolly Lutz Morris' first paper-mache building was an enchanted cottage, which she draped with roses as if the fairies had come the night before to adorn it. The cottages were very popular in Dolly's shop, and soon a teacher saw it and requested a custom-made "enchanted schoolhouse."

To form the armature for the schoolhouse, cut a rectangle from foam that's 3.5 inches wide x 3 inches deep x 5 inches high (9 x 7.5 x 12 cm) at the roof's peak with the side walls 3.5 inches high. Then cut another rectangle of foam measuring 1.5 inches wide x 1 inch deep x 2 inches high (4 x 2.5 x 5 cm) for the steeple, cutting the peak of the steeple's roof so the side walls are 1.5 inches high. Cut a V-notch in the bottom of the steeple to match the peak of the main building's roof and glue the steeple to the center of the building.

Form a base of gray instant paper-mache measuring 1/4 inch thick x 5 inches wide x 4.5 inches deep (6 mm x 12 cm x 11.5 cm). Place the foam armature on top of the base so the back of the schoolhouse lines up with the back of the base. Cover the walls of the house with a layer of mache using a butter knife, taking care to blend the mache into the base so they will adhere. Use the blade of the knife to press in the shapes of bricks, a door, and windows.

Enchanted School House

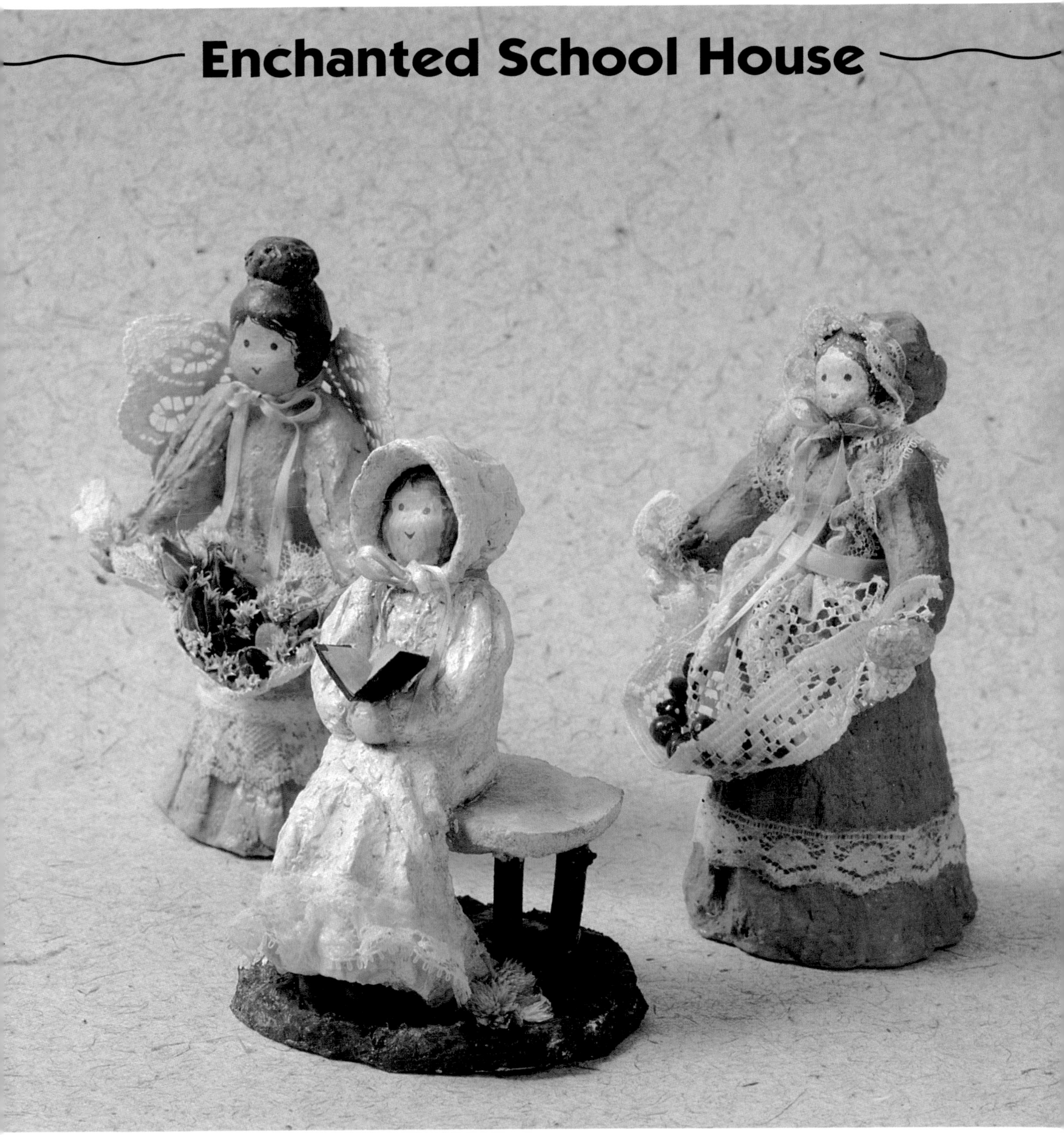

Cover the roof and steeple areas with mache, and then press brick shapes into the steeple area. Create the illusion of a stone wall by attaching five 1-inch-diameter circles of mache to the side of the base and manipulating them until their shapes are irregular. Form the steps leading up to the front door with three rectangles of mache mixture.

After all of the mache completely dries, apply a layer of acrylic gesso, then paint with acrylics. The natural gray color of the mache makes an attractive touch for the stones and steps, so you may not want to paint these areas. Finish decorating the cottage by gluing on moss, small cones, and fragrant dried herbs.

Little Angel, Apron Girl, and Rachel

Dolly adapted the designs for these figurines from historical porcelain figurines that were trimmed with stiffened lace. Building them over an armature (a base) instead of from solid mache allows Dolly to create a wider range of poses and decorations.

For Little Angel, first form an armature by making a poster board cone that's 6 inches high x 2 inches in diameter (15 x 5 cm) and tape it together. Cut a 6-inch piece of heavy-gauge floral wire and tape its center to the cone 1.25 inches (13 mm) below the cone's point to form the top of the shoulders.

Next, cover the cone from the wire down with a 1/2-inch (12 mm) thick layer of mache. Use the rounded end of a metal nail file to press in the skirt ruffles and allow the mache to completely dry before continuing with the next step. Add a 1.25-inch ball of mache above the shoulders to form the head, blending it in with the shoulders. Blend a 1/2-inch ball of mache on top of the head to form a hair bun, and indent the eye area with the round end of a metal nail file. Allow this portion of the angel to completely dry before continuing.

Add a 2-inch coil of mache over each wire to form the arms, carefully blending it into the body. Use the nail file to add drapes to the sleeves, and then curl up the hands in a spoon shape to hold the lace draper. After the mache completely dries, apply a coat of acrylic gesso. When it dries, add color with acrylics, apply a coat of clear acrylic sealant, apply a coat of antiquing medium, and finish with another coat of sealant, allowing each layer to completely dry before adding the next

To form the wings, dip a 3.5- x 2-inch (9 x 5 cm) piece of lace in fabric stiffener and allow it to dry flat on a piece of plastic. Glue the lace to the back of the angel. Next glue a narrow piece of gathered lace around the bottom of the skirt for a ruf-fle. To form the drape, gather both ends of a 6- x 2-inch rectangle of lace and tie both ends off with thread 1/2 inch from the end. Glue the ends of the lace to the angel's hands and the middle of her body, and fill the drape with dried flowers. Last, glue a small satin bow under the angel's chin.

For the Apron Girl, form a poster board armature with the same techniques as for the Little Angel. Mark the waist area with a pencil mark 4 inches (10 cm) from the bottom of the cone and cover the cone from this mark down with a 1/2-inch-thick layer of mache to form the skirt. Then press ruffles into the skirt with the rounded end of a metal nail file. After this layer of mache completely dries, cover the cone from the waist to the top of the shoulders with a 1/4-inch-thick layer of mache to form the torso.

Press on a 1.25-inch ball of mache above the shoulders to form the head, and then add a 1-inch ball of mache at the back of the head for the bonnet, blending the bonnet mache into the head with care and adding fabric gathers with a nail file. After this mache completely dries, bend the arm wires to their proper positions and cover each one with a 2.25-inch-long (5.5 cm) coil of mache. Form the hands into a spoon shape so they will look like they're holding both ends of the apron.

After adding gesso, acrylic paint, spray sealant, antiquing medium, and another coat of spray sealant (allowing plenty of drying time between each coat), glue a narrow piece of gathered lace around the bottom of the skirt and glue lace around the face to form the bonnet's brim. For the top of the apron, glue a piece of lace from the waist up over the shoulders and back down to the waist. For the bottom of the apron, gather a 3- x 7-inch (7.5 x 17 cm) rectangle of lace to 1.5 inches at the long top and tie off with a knot. Glue the apron to the Apron Girl's waist and glue the apron ends to her hands. To finish, glue a narrow ribbon bow under her chin and a 10-inch (25 cm) length of ribbon around the waist for the waistband, tying it in a bow in the back. Last, fill the apron with rose hip berries or other colorful dried flowers.

To make the seated doll, Rachel, first construct the bench by rolling out a rectangle of mache that's 1.5 x 2.5 x 1/4 inch thick and inserting a 1.5- x 1/4-inch twig into each corner for legs. Leave the bench upside down until it's completely dry. Make another mache base 3.75 inches wide x 3.25 inches deep x 1/4 inch thick (9.5 cm x 8 cm x 6 mm), and insert the legs of the bench into the mache so that the back of the bench is even with the back of the base.

After the bench completely dries, make a poster board cone for the torso base measuring 3 inches tall with a 1-inch diameter. Place the cone in the middle of the bench and cover the cone 2 inches up from the bottom with a thin layer of mache. The top inch of the cone will become Rachel's head. To form the lower portion of the doll, make a poster board cone measuring 3 inches tall x 2 inches in diameter. Bend the cone in half to form the doll's knees and place it on the base with the point facing her torso and the cone's bottom at the base in front of the bench. Cover the cone with mache to form the skirt. Using the rounded end of a metal nail file, press in drapes of the skirt. Do not continue working until this section completely dries.

Cover the top of the torso cone with a 1-inch ball of mache to create Rachel's face. Add more mache to the back of her head to make the puffy bonnet crown and allow it to completely dry. Then add a flattened roll of mache around her face to form the bonnet's brim and blend it in with the back of the bonnet. To form the arms and hands, roll out two 3-inch coils and attach one to each shoulder, bending down half way for the elbows and allowing the hands to meet in the center of her lap. Create a book cover by folding a 1- x 2-inch rectangle of poster board in half and placing it in Rachel's hands, indenting the book as needed for a secure fit. Remove the book and glue several paper pages in it while the mache is drying.

When the piece is completely dry, paint with acrylics. Position the book back in Rachel's hands and glue it in place. Glue a lace ruffle to the bottom of the dress and glue a bow under her chin. After the paint dries, apply a clear layer of aerosol sealant, a coat of antiquing medium, and finish with another layer of sealant, allowing each layer to completely dry before adding the next. As a final touch, glue some dried flowers onto the bench. ❖

Rhino & Elephant

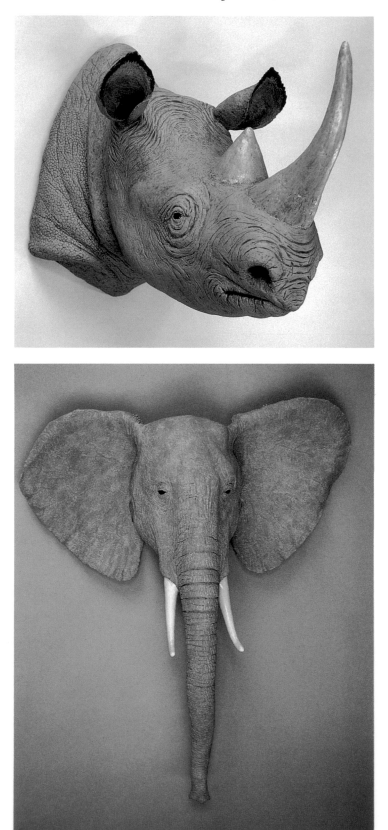

Wild animals have intrigued sculptor Lucas Adams all his life, but it wasn't until eight or nine years ago that he began creating his animals from instant paper-mache.

First create a base from a large block of foam, carving it down with a serrated kitchen knife until you're happy with the rough form. Finish shaping the base with sandpaper and apply a thin coat of grey mache. When the mache dries, add several more layers, allowing each one to completely dry before adding the next, and adding more and more detail with each layer of mache.

Press glass eyes into the mache. (Lucas uses taxidermists as a good source for realistic-looking eyes, although you can find them in a craft supply store if you're not as concerned with verisimilitude.) Then sand the teeth to remove any roughness. To remove any roughness from the facial area, apply a layer of acrylic gesso, allow it to dry, and then sand more if needed. Attach a plastic insert on the back side for hanging with epoxy. When you're happy with the texture of the face, apply a layer of acrylic gesso and allow it to dry. Then apply several coats of gesso-diluted acrylic paint, using a small brush for the hair areas and a larger brush for the facial areas. ❖

Paper-Mache Zoo

Sculptor and multi-media artist Lucas Adams creates bases for these wonderfully shaped animals from chicken wire and stiffened fabric, instead of with carved foam like the animals on page 58.

First make the base by forming the rough shape from 1-inch (2.5 cm) chicken wire and then cover the base with plaster wrap. After the wrap dries, cover the base with several thin layers of instant paper-mache, allowing the mache to dry between layers and creating more detail with each succeeding layer.

After the last layer of mache dries, apply a coat of two-part urethane foam inside the base to strengthen the tusks, trunk, and horn. Apply a length of steel cable to the back for the hanger while you're working with the urethane. Position and attach two glass eyes. Gesso and sand the pieces until you achieve a satisfactory smoothness, allowing the gesso to dry before each sanding. For the rhino, paint the face with gesso-diluted acrylics to achieve a matte finish, and paint the horn with gloss paint for a natural look. For the elephant, apply color with oil paint, and then spray on a layer of clear urethane as a finish after the paint is completely dry. ❖

Lion & Tiger

Frog Fancy

Designer Mary Beth Ruby does not use sandpaper or spend excessive amounts of time smoothing the surface of her animal figures because she believes that the rough texture of instant paper-mache makes very realistic skin.

First cut out a piece of instant paper-mache in the shape of a lily pad. Place the lily pad on a drying rack and do not turn it over during the drying process so that the edges will curl up.

Bunny Girl

To form the frog's body, arrange wads of newspaper over a toilet paper roll, taping as needed and adding more paper until you're happy with the general shape of the body.

Next, cut strips of newsprint measuring 3 inches x 7 inches (7.5 x 18 cm) for the front claws and strips measuring 4 inches x 7 inches (10 x 18 cm) for the back claws. Roll the strips into tubes and tape them in place. Then insert a length of clothesline wire in and out of each tube until you have enough for each foot. Spread the claws out at one end and tape them close together at the other end. Repeat until you have two front feet and two back feet. Attach the feet in place with a short length of floral wire, and tightly twist the wire ends to secure.

Cover the body and front feet with mache first. Add extra mache on the face for the eyeballs, and press in a mouth with a plastic knife. Position the frog on the lily pad and begin covering the back feet with mache, blending the two areas of mache with care so they will look natural and adhere together. After the mache completely dries, prime the frog with a layer of gesso. Then paint with acrylics, and finish with a layer of clear varnish, allowing each coat to completely dry before adding the next. ❖

Designer Dolly Lutz Morris has always found children in footed pajamas to be adorable, and one of her own toddlers inspired this figurine. First form the doll's armature by folding and taping a piece of poster board into a cylinder measuring 1/2 inch in diameter and 6 inches (13 mm x 15 cm) tall. Form an oval base of instant paper-mache measuring 2.5 inches wide x 2 inches deep x 1/4 inch thick (6.5 cm x 5 cm x 6 mm). Press the cylinder into the mache base and allow it to thoroughly dry.

Mark the cone with a pencil 4 inches (10 cm) up from the base to indicate the top shoulders area. Cover the cylinder with a thin layer of mache from this mark downward and allow the mache to completely dry. To form an armature for the ears, fold two 6-inch lengths of medium-gauge floral wire into an M shape. Tape the bottom wires together and then tape them to the top back of the cylinder. Cover the wire with a thin layer of mache, creating indents for the center of the ears with the pointed end of a metal nail file. Allow the ears to thoroughly dry before continuing to the next step.

Add additional mache to form the feet and legs, and add more mache in the tummy and chest area to make a rounded belly. Roll out two 2-inch-long (5 cm) coils to form the arms and hands and press them in place. Indent the area where the

hands and sleeves meet with the nail file. Curve two 1.5-inch pieces of wire together to form a basket handle and press them into the mache between the hands. Allow the figurine to completely dry before continuing to the next step.

To form the basket, flatten a 1-inch (2.5 cm) ball of mache and shape it into a basket. Blend the basket into the body of the girl and into the basket handle wire in the front. Add texture to the basket with the nail file by pressing in crisscross lines of basket weave and allow to completely dry. Form two small eggs from the mache and allow to dry separately.

Seal the figure with a layer of acrylic gesso, allow it to completely dry, and then paint the figure with acrylics. Glue a small bit of moss into the basket and then glue the eggs onto the moss. Glue a small bow under the doll's chin. Apply a layer of clear spray sealant, then a layer of antiquing medium, and finish with a final layer of spray sealant, allowing each coat to completely dry before adding the next. ❖

Designer Dolly Lutz Morris frequently gives throwaway dolls new life by recycling their body parts into new dolls. For this project, Dolly was thrilled to be able to create a pretty new look for one of her cherished childhood dolls.

Make a cone from poster board measuring 3 inches (7.5 cm) at the diameter with a height that's as tall as the distance from the feet to the waist of a purchased 7.5-inch doll (18 cm) with enough width at the top to accommodate her waist. Tape the cone to the doll's waist and then tape the cone's sides securely together. Work on a plastic plate for ease in turning the project.

Cut out the robe as directed in the sidebar on page 77. Cut the center back fold open and then stitch the side and under-arm seams with a 1/4-inch (6 mm) seam allowance. Dip the robe in fabric stiffener, wring out any excess, and place it on the doll. Secure the back opening shut with rust-proof sewing pins and turn under the fabric's bottom edge. Arrange the robe in folds and pin in place. Then tie a piece of thread around the waist to create the waistline. Allow the fabric to completely dry before continuing.

Country Angel

For the apron, cut out a rectangle of striped fabric measuring 4 x 8 inches (10 x 20 cm). Hem the bottom 8-inch edge and sew a row of gathering stitches. Gather the hem to 3 inches (7.5 cm), and tie off the thread with a knot. Dip the fabric in stiffener, wring out any excess, and then pin the gathered edge to the robe's waist area. Gather the apron corners 1 inch from the bottom side of each edge with a stitch and tack them to the edges of the doll's sleeves to create a pocket for the apples. Shape the pocket and drape of the apron, and then allow it to completely dry.

For the wings, cut two lace wing shapes from the pattern shown below. Dip the wings in stiffener and place them flat on a piece of plastic wrap to dry. Then glue an 18-inch (46 cm) length of ivory ribbon around the doll's waist at the top of the apron and tie in a bow in the back. Glue a red bow with long streamers at her neck. To finish, glue three plastic apples in the apron and one on her skirt. ❖

Christmas Cheer

Dollmaker Dolly Lutz Morris gets a special thrill from making these stiffened fabric dolls. Compared with her paper-mache Santas, (see page XX), the fabric forms go together remarkably fast because you don't have to sculpt any details. The angel is a special project for Dolly because she was able to recycle a childhood doll whose clothing had been lost over the years.

Woodland Father Christmas

Form a secure base for the figure by filling the bottom of a 22-ounce liquid dish detergent bottle with sand or pebbles. Glue a 2-3/8- x 1-7/8-inch (6 x 4.7 cm) foam egg onto the bottle's neck to form the head, and glue a 2-inch (5 cm) square of cheesecloth over the egg to form the face. When the glue has dried, apply two more coats of glue over the cheesecloth with a paint brush.

To form the arms, wrap the middle of an 18-inch (46 cm) length of heavy-gauge floral wire around the middle of the neck, allowing about 6 inches (15 cm) to protrude on each side. Cover the wire with tape to prevent it from rusting later and staining the fabric. Bend the arm wires downward, allowing 2

inches for the shoulder area. For the mittens, cut four pieces of suede cloth, each measuring 2 inches long x 1.5 inches wide (5 x 4 cm). Round the mitten shape with scissors on one of the small sides, then stitch a 1/4-inch (6 mm) seam on the two long and one rounded side. Turn right sides out and fill the mittens with polyester stuffing. Pull the mittens over the end of the arm wire and tie them onto the wire at the wrist with twine. Build up the arms and shoulders with polyester stuffing, winding twine around the outside as you work to secure the padding in place as you work.

Cut out the robe as directed in the sidebar on page 77. Cut up the middle of the center front for the robe's opening and then stitch the side and under-arm seams with a 1/4-inch seam allowance. Dip the robe in fabric stiffener, wring out any excess, and place it over the bottle. Place the robe on the Santa with the opening in front and turn under the bottom edge. Arrange drapes and folds in the fabric, securing them in place with rust-proof sewing pins until dry. Pin the front opening shut except at the very bottom, and allow the fabric to thoroughly dry before continuing.

Add the skin color and facial

expressions with acrylic paint. Then cut several lengths of craft fur into 3/4-inch (20 mm) wide strips and glue them around the trim areas. Hold the fur in place with pins until dry. Glue wool doll hair in place for the hair and beard, and then glue on several shorter lengths of doll hair for the eyebrows and mustache. Spray all of the hair with hair spray and fluff to shape.

Next, glue an 11-inch (27 cm) twig in the figure's extended hand and a small basket in the other hand. Glue a circle of artificial greens on the head for a garland. Decorate the basket, staff, and garland by gluing on small cones, berries, dried flowers, and greens.

Victorian Angel

Construct a cardboard cone measuring 8.5 inches high and 3.5 inches wide (21 x 9 cm) at the base, adjusting the cone as needed so its top will fit over the waist of a 7.5-inch (18 cm) purchased doll. The cone will add height and elegance to the angel, as well as provide a form for the fabric to drape over. Tape or glue the top of the cone to the doll's torso.

Cut out the robe as directed in the sidebar on page 77. Cut up the center front fold so the robe can be fitted on the doll,

and sew the underarm and side seams with a 1/4-inch seam allowance. Dip the robe in fabric stiffener, wring out any excess, and place it on the doll with the center opening down the back. Arrange folds and drapes in the fabric, using rust-proof sewing pins to hold the fabric in place until it dries, and turn the rough edge at the bottom under. Tie a 1/2-inch (13 mm) gold ribbon around the waist. Pin the back center opening shut and allow the fabric to completely dry before continuing.

Cut the wings out of poster board, noting the fold placement on the pattern. Glue lace over both sides of the poster board and trim off any excess fabric after the glue dries. Paint the wings with gold acrylic paint, allow to thoroughly dry, and then glue the wings in place on the back side of the angel. To form the ribbon drapes, dip a length of narrow burgundy ribbon in fabric stiffener. Pin the ribbon at the shoulder and begin twisting and turning it downward for a flowing effect, holding it in place where needed with pins

until the ribbon dries. Repeat with narrow gold ribbon and again with a wider gold and mauve ribbon, crossing the ribbons in the chest area and draping them over her shoulders and down the center of the wings in the back. Cut the ribbon ends in points, and then glue a circle of gold thread to the angel's hair for a halo. ❖

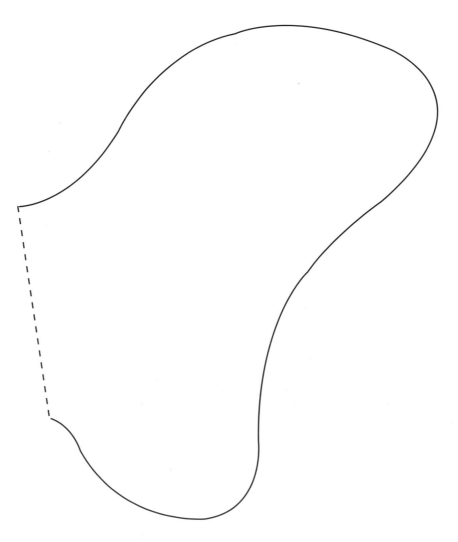

Victorian Santa

Mary Beth Ruby uses old thread cones or foam cones as the base for her Victorian Santas.

First roll out a sheet of instant paper-mache as described on page 10. Lay the cone sideways on top of the mache. Form the mache around the cone with dampened fingertips, smoothing the surface as you work. Trim off the excess mache from the bottom of the cone, and shape the top point into a Santa hat.

After the mache dries for at least a day (it doesn't have to be completely dry), make the Santa's arms with a roll of pulp and press them in place. Next, form Santa's hat fur and the trim pieces on his coat, and press them in place. Shape Santa's beard and nose from small pieces of pulp, using old pens, toothpicks, small clay tools, or anything else that's handy to add texture.

After the mache completely dries, seal it with gesso and then paint with acrylics. Create an antiqued look to the Santa by diluting burnt umber acrylic paint with water until it's very thin, and then brushing it over the entire Santa. While the paint is still wet, rub most of it off with a soft cloth or paper towel. Seal the Santa with a coat of varnish after the paint completely dries. ❖

Crocheted Angels

rafter Diane Shelton enjoys sharing her stiffened crochet projects at shows with fellow crafters. In addition to her popular angels, Diane also makes tree ornaments, baby shower gifts, and window decorations. To make the angels, dip the crocheted shapes (see sidebar for crochet instructions) into fabric stiffener and arrange them over a foam cone to dry. Decorate with craft pearls, ribbon bows, and a halo made from a metalic pipe cleaner. ❖

Treetop Angel

Row 1. Ch. 5 10 hdc in circle. 2. 2 hdc in each hdc. 3. hdc in each hdc. 4, 5, 6, 7, 8. Repeat row 3. 9. * hdc in 1st hdc skip next hdc* repeat. 10. Ch. 4 dc in 1st hdc dc ch. 1 dc in each hdc (Vst) 11, 12, 13, 14, 15. Vst in each Vst around. 16. Ch. 4 trp. ch. 1 2 trp. in Vst * 2 trp. ch. 1 2 trp* in each Vst around. 17, 18, 19. Repeat row 16. 20-23. *2 trp ch. 1 2 trp. ch. 1 * repeat around. 24-26. * 2 trp. ch. 2 2 trp. ch. 1* repeat. 27. * 2 trp. ch. 2 2 trp. ch. 2. * repeat. 28. In shell work * 5 trp. picot 5 trp. ch. 1 sc between shells * repeat around. ARMS. Row 1. Ch. 4 12 dc in chain. 2. Ch 4 tr in next dc. ch. 1. * trp in next 2 dc ch. 1* repeat. 3-5. Repeat row 2. 6. *trp. in each trp. ch. 2 between. * repeat. 7. Repeat 6. 8. * sc in 1st 2 trp. 2sc in ch. * repeat. 9. Trp. ch. 1 in each sp. 10. skip into 1st ch. 1 sp. ch. 5 slip st into 3 ch. dc in same sp. * dc ch. 3 slip st. in top of dc, dc in same sp. * repeat. Wings. Row 1. Ch. 4 2dc * ch. 2 2dc* repeat 3 times. 2. Shell in 1st 2 spaces ch. 1 sc between. 2dc ch. 1 shell in next shell. 3. Ch. 3 dc ch. 2 dc ch. 2 dc in 1st shell shell in next ch. 1 sp. sc in sc. shell in next 2 shells. 4. Ch. 3 shell in next 2 space ch. 1 sc in shell in next 3 shells. 5. Double shell in 1st shell (2dc ch. 1 2dc ch. 1 2dc) shell across with sc in sc double-shell in last shell. 6. Even shells across. 7. Double shell in 1st shell * shells across with ch. 1 sc between *. 8. Even shells. 9. Double-shell even shells across till last shell then double-shell. 10. Shell even. 11. Double-shell in 1st shell then even shells across. 12. Even shells. Finish. Stiffen angel on cone, wings dry flat, stuff arms with plastic wrap then pin to angel top. let dry and decorate.

Small Angel

Row 1. Ch. 4. join 6 sc in circle. 2. 1sc in 1st st. 2sc in next. repeat around don't join. 3. 1 sc in 1st then 2sc in next around. 4-6. Repeat row 3. 7-8. sc in 1st st. skip next continue until only 7 st. are left. 9. Ch. 4 dc in 1st st. * dc ch. 1 dc in next st.* repeat. 7 Vst. 10. skip to 1st st. Vst in Vst and in space between (14 Vst). 11.* Vst in Vst dc between Vst* repeat around. 12. Slip into 1st st. Ch. 4 dc in same st. Vst in Vst. Vst in next dc Vst in Vst. skip 5dc and 5 Vst. in next dc work one Vst, Vst in next Vst, Vst in dc, Vst in Vst, skip next 5 dc and 5Vst. join to 1st Vst. 13 and 14. Slip into 1st make shell in each Vst. 14.* shell ch. 1 shell * repeat. 15.* Shell ch. 2.Shell* repeat. 16.* Shell (2dc ch.2 2dc) ch2 shell*. repeat. 17. *Shell 3dc picot 3dc, ch. 1 sc between shells ch.1 picot shell * repeat.

Wings. Join at waist in dc ch. * 2 dc ch.1, 2 dc in Vst ch.2 sc in dc.* Repeat till you have 5 scallops. Make other wing the same way. Stiffen angel over cone.

Christmas Cottage & Roly-Poly Santa

Dollmaker Dolly Lutz Morris fashioned this instant paper mache Santa after the Roly Poly tin tobacco containers that appeared around 1900. Inspiration for the Christmas Cottage came from the paper mache buildings her mother used to make to decorate the train set under their Christmas tree.

To form a base for the cottage walls, first cut out a rectangle of floral foam measuring 4 inches wide x 3 inches deep x 4 inches high (10 x 7.5 x 10 cm). Then cut out and glue a triangle of foam measuring 3 inches at its base and 2 inches high to the top of the rectangle to form the roof peak. Cut out and glue a 1-inch-wide x 1.5-inch-deep x 7-inch-high (2.5 x 4 x 17 cm) rec-

tangle of foam to the middle side for the chimney. Bend a 3- x 1.5-inch piece of cardboard into an inverted V-shape and tape it to the middle front of the cottage just below the roof shape to form the roof over the door.

Make an oval of mache for the base that's 1/4 inch thick x 7 inches wide x 4.5 inches (6 mm x 17 cm x 11.5 cm) deep. Place the cottage form on the base with the back of the cottage at the back of the oval. Use a butter knife to cover the cottage walls with a layer of mache, blending it into the base so the two will stick together. Press in brick, door, and window shapes with a knife blade. Next, cover the roof area with mache, keeping the surface uneven so it will look like snow, and then cover the door roof with mache.

To form the chimney, cover the chimney base with mache and then use the side of a knife to press in mortarlike impressions around the stones. Create a snow-covered chimney effect by spreading an uneven layer of mache over the chimney. Next, make six 1-inch circles of mache and press them into the chimney's side base edge to create the look of a stone wall, shaping the stones into irregular shapes as you work.

———

After the mache completely dries, prime the surface with a layer of gesso and then paint with acrylics. After the paint dries, glue on finishing details such as a small silk pine tree, pine boughs on the roof, pieces of pine, hemlock cones, rose hip berries, and dried flowers.

———

For the Santa, cover a 3-inch foam ball with a 1/2-inch thick layer of mache. At the top, add a 1.5-inch ball of mache to create the rough head shape. After the mache completely dries, roll out two coils of mache that are 1.75 inches thick and 4 inches long for the arms. Press the coils in place, bending them at the elbows, and then add 1/2-inch balls for gloves. Scoop the right hand so it can hold the bird, and mold the left hand so it will look like it's clutching the wreath. Next, add extra mache at the end of the sleeves and down the front of the Santa for the fur trim.

———

To add detail to Santa's head, shape the nose out of a small triangle of mache and the cheeks out of two small balls, pressing the shapes in place and blending them in with the base mache. Build up the fore-head shape with a rectangle of mache, leaving the eye areas indented, and add a crescent shape for the mouth. After this mache completely dries, add more mache for hair and a beard, creating texture

with the pointed end of a metal nail file. Next, press two small coils of mache in place for the eyebrows and a longer coil in place for the mustache. Create texture as you did with the beard.

———

After all of the mache dries, paint, seal, antique, and seal again, allowing each coat to

completely dry before adding the next. After the final coat of sealant dries, glue a garland of silk greens around Santa's head, and decorate the gar-land with small berries, cones, and pieces of dried flowers. Then glue another decorated circle of silk greens to Santa's left hand and a small bird in his right hand. ❖

Easter Bunnies

Designer Dottie Shultz has made a lot of improvements in her bunny-making techniques over the years. Her first rabbits, made many years ago, didn't even stand up straight! Primarily a painter, Dottie derives the most pleasure from adding the painted details to her paper-mache pieces, and her Easter rabbits are one of the most popular holiday items in her gift shop.

Start a rabbit with two foam eggs, one 3 inches (7.5 cm) and one 5 inches (12 cm). Cut a slice off the large end of the 5-inch egg and insert two toothpicks partway into the top of the egg. Place the small egg sideways onto the small egg. The larger end of the small egg will become the back of the rabbit's head.

Completely cover the form with a thin layer of mache. Smooth the mache with dampened fingers to save work later on. To form the ears, insert three toothpicks for each ear into the top of the head in a triangle formation, tilting the toothpicks slightly forward and making the ends come together. Cover each triangle of toothpicks with a 3- x 3/4-inch (7.5 cm x 20 mm) tube of mache, and use a dampened brush to smooth the areas where the mache joins and the ears.

To form the face, make two balls of mache about the size of large lima beans. Place them side by side, just above the small end of the egg, to form the cheeks. Add a small flat piece of mache at the bottom of the cheeks where the two balls meet to form a mouth, and then use a dampened brush to smooth the joined areas together. Form another piece of mache into an arrowhead shape and place it on the head and the cheeks with the pointy end between the cheek balls and the flat end between the ears. Again, work the joined areas together with a dampened brush. Use the pointy end of a toothpick to form a ball for the nose, and shape the flat end into a forehead, working it over to the ears. When the shape looks right, use your thumbs to form two eye sockets where the arrowhead widens.

To form the arms, make two ropes of mache with one end slightly narrowed for the paws. Press the arms gently in place, shaping their shoulders so they blend back into the body. Adjust their length if necessary, and work the joined areas together with a dampened brush. Form a thumb on the top of each paw with a toothpick. (Note: If you'd prefer one of the arms to extend outward,

position it as you like and then insert a toothpick through the paw and into the body to hold it in position until the mache dries.)

Add the feet next, keeping them a little off to the sides and using a toothpick to score the toes. To form the tail, attach a ball of mache to the lower center back, and work the mache together with a damp brush. Create furlike impressions in the tail with the wide end of a toothpick.

To form Mrs. Rabbit's scarf, roll out a small sheet of mache and cut out a triangle from it. Arrange the triangle around the rabbit's neck and add pieces of mache to bring the scarf together in the front. Next, add a small ball for the knot and two pieces to create the illusion of the scarf coming out of the knot, and work the joined areas together with a dampened brush. Create the illusion of folds in the scarf by scoring the mache with the wooden end of a paint brush. Next, use a dampened brush to smooth and shape the scarf. When the folds look natural, take a larger brush and go over the scarf, and then use a toothpick to make fringe on the edge of the scarf. To create the fur fluff around the bunny's neck, push small

pieces of mache in place.

Use the wooden handle of a paint brush to score a fabric pattern for Mr. Rabbit's scarf into the mache. Use a dampened brush to smooth the mache below the scarf so it looks like the scarf is on top of the rabbit's body.

Carefully check for and fix any fingerprints that might be on the rabbits, and place them on a cake rack to dry. Apply a coat of acrylic gesso, and then paint on a base coat of brown acrylic, followed by a lighter color of brown applied randomly over the fur to create natural-looking highlights. Next, paint the jacket, scarf, and facial features, and then brush on a little blush highlight on the cheeks and the inner ears. After all the acrylic paint dries, apply a light layer of clear acrylic spray, a coat of water-based antiquing medium, and finish with a final layer of clear acrylic spray, allowing each coat to completely dry before adding the next. ❖

Scary Friends

Dottie Shultz's customers love buying small knick-knacks to bring some holiday spirit into their homes. Dottie says that instant paper-mache projects store well from one season to the next, as long as they are wrapped in a few protective layers of paper or fabric; in extremely humid areas, Dottie recommends adding a packet of moisture-absorbing silica gel to the storage box.

Sitting Pumpkin

First cover a light bulb with a layer of mache, making the mache thicker on the round area of the bulb. Then press the top of the bulb against a flat surface so the pumpkin will sit flat. (If your mache isn't sticking well to the glass surface, allow your first, uncooperative layer to dry, and then mold a fresh layer of mache over the first to smooth out any problem areas.)

To create the hat, add more mache to the small end of the bulb and shape it into a point. Then roll some mache into a 5- x 1/2-inch (12 cm x 13 mm) tube and press the tube in place about 3 inches (7.5 cm) down from the hat's point. Use a dampened brush to seal the joining area, and then use your dampened fingers to form a hat brim. To make the pumpkin look more realistic, make five or six score lines from top to bottom with a toothpick. For the pumpkin's face, use a toothpick and bristle brush to form triangles for the eyes and nose and an opening for the mouth.

Pumpkin Ghost

Form the beginning of the base by gluing a wooden popsicle stick about halfway through the center of a 4-inch (10 cm) foam cone. Fold two paper towels (the more expensive brands work better) in half diagonally and then in half again. From the center point, mark off 4 inches around the bottom and tear the towels along the marks to form an 8-inch (20 cm) circle. Brush the towels with a light coating of fabric stiffener on both sides and make a small slit in the center of each towel. Place one towel over the top of the cone, with the popsicle stick protruding through the cut in the towel's center, and arrange the towel in folds around the cone.

Next, insert a toothpick into each side at the top of the cone to support the arms. The rounded toothpick ends should face the outside and angle slightly upward. Place the second towel over the cone and arrange it in folds. After the towels dry, press a 1.5- or 2-inch (4 to 5 cm) foam ball onto the stick to form a hole for later attachment and remove the ball. Then cover the ball with a layer of mache and place it back onto the stick, but not all the way down to the towels, to finish shaping. Form a small ball of mache into a stem and place it on top of the pumpkin, using a dampened brush to seal the area where the mache joins. Score indentations from top to bottom around the pumpkin face, avoiding the area where the facial expressions will be painted. After sealing and painting, remove the pumpkin's head, fill the hole three-fourths full with glue, and then reinsert the head.

Rosie the Witch

Begin the witch by covering a 9-inch (22 cm) foam cone with a layer of mache. Push a toothpick about 1/2 inch (12 mm) down into the top of the cone and cover it with mache to form a pointy hat. For the hat's brim, make a 4- x 1/2-inch (10 cm x 12 mm) tube of mache and position it about 3 inches (7.5 cm) down from the hat's point, sealing it at the base with a dampened brush. Shape the tube into the brim with your dampened fingers, taking care to not let the rim get too wet.

For the witches's hair, add small pieces of mache under the hat and around the head, and cre-

ate fringes with a toothpick so the hair looks stringy. For the face, push into the mache with a toothpick to form the eyebrows and nose. Smooth the face and finish shaping with a dampened brush. Then add more mache to the chin area create a pointy chin with your fingers and a brush. For the cape, press pieces of mache down both sides of the front and around the bottom, and shape the cape's edges over the dress. For added detail, create raised areas around the

back of the dress to look like fabric folds.

———

Now form the hands and position them so they appear to be coming out from under the cape. They should meet and overlap at the center of the dress. Seal the meeting areas with a damp brush. Next, make a hole behind the hands to insert the broom, allowing a little extra space so the hole will still be large enough after shrinkage.

Finishing

After finishing the pieces, check them carefully for fingerprints and rough spots, and place them on a cake rack and allow them to completely dry. Then brush on a sealing layer of acrylic gesso, paint with acrylics, apply a layer of aerosol sealant, then a layer of antiquing medium, and finish with another coat of sealant, allowing each coat to completely dry before adding the next. ❖

Black Cats

These black cats make the perfect partners for Dottie Shultz's witches on page 73. To create the base for each cat, first slice a small piece off the large end of a 3-inch (7.5 cm) foam egg. Next, cut a 2-inch (5 cm) foam ball in half and slice off one edge. Dip the ends of two toothpicks in craft glue and insert them partway into the lower side of the egg. (See illustration.) Then dip the extending tips in glue and insert them into the half ball with the flat side toward the egg. Dip the ends of two more toothpicks in glue and insert them in the top of the egg to form a tail.

Cover the foam shapes with a layer of instant paper-mache. Cover the tail by forming a 3-inch tube of mache, slipping it over the toothpicks, and smoothing the mache together at the joining areas. Shape the protruding portion of the mache tube upward to form a curved tail. To form the face, make two pea-sized balls for the cheeks and press them against the bottom of the head. Next, add a small piece of mache across the bottom of the balls where they meet to create the mouth. Then add another tiny ball of mache to form the nose.

For the ears, press two balls of mache about the size of a lima bean around your thumb and squeeze one end to a point. Press them in place and smooth the areas where the mache surfaces meet. For the paws, flatten two more balls about the size of a lima bean into paw shapes, press them in place, and smooth the areas where the surfaces meet. After the cat completely dries, apply a coat of acrylic gesso and allow it to dry before beginning to paint.

To finish the cat, apply two coats of black acrylic paint and then paint the eyes and whiskers in a white acrylic paint that has been mixed with just a dab of black. After the acrylics dry, seal with a layer of aerosol spray, antique, and finish with another layer of sealant, allowing each coat to completely dry before continuing with the next. ❖

Doll Robes: Patterns and Cutting Instructions

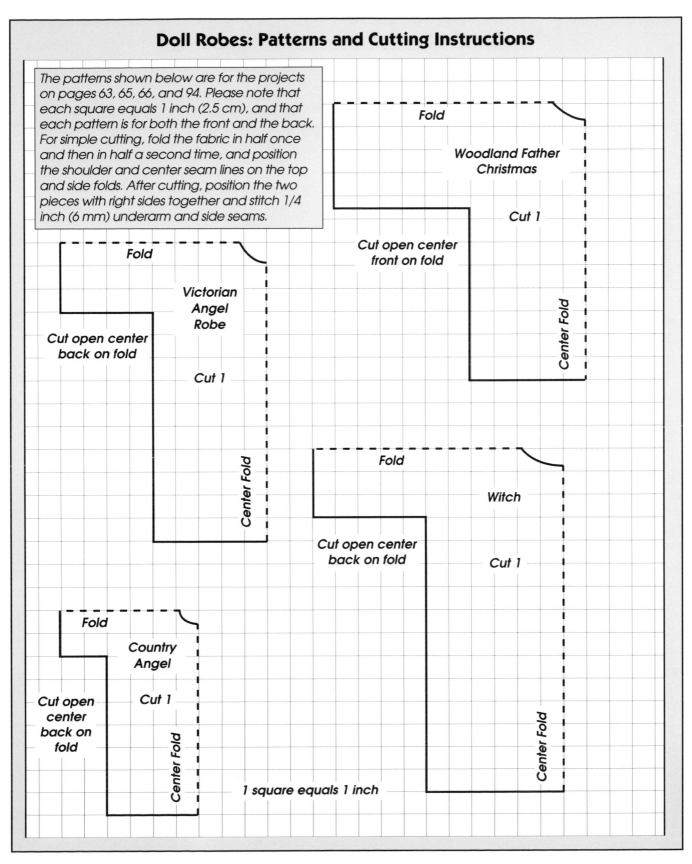

The patterns shown below are for the projects on pages 63, 65, 66, and 94. Please note that each square equals 1 inch (2.5 cm), and that each pattern is for both the front and the back. For simple cutting, fold the fabric in half once and then in half a second time, and position the shoulder and center seam lines on the top and side folds. After cutting, position the two pieces with right sides together and stitch 1/4 inch (6 mm) underarm and side seams.

Fold

Woodland Father Christmas

Cut 1

Cut open center front on fold

Center Fold

Fold

Victorian Angel Robe

Cut open center back on fold

Cut 1

Center Fold

Fold

Witch

Cut open center back on fold

Cut 1

Center Fold

Fold

Country Angel

Cut 1

Cut open center back on fold

Center Fold

1 square equals 1 inch

CHILDHOOD ENDEARMENTS

Tea Party

Designer Anne McCloskey created this colorful ensemble of paper-mache confections and props for tea parties and special celebration occasions. Form the cupcakes by dipping 12 to 14 strips of torn newsprint into a mache mixture. Wad the newspaper into a shape to fill the inside of a foil cupcake baking cup. Next, press and mold the mache on top of the cup until it's flat. After the mache dries, paint it with a solid acrylic color, then create sprinkles with dots and dashes in dimensional fabric paint.

To form the tea cups, apply a layer of petroleum jelly to the inside of a glass tea cup. Follow with several layers of newspaper mache and allow it to dry. After the outside of the cup is partially dry, remove it from the glass cup and allow it to finish drying. Next, cut out a strip of cardboard to form the handle and tape it to the cup. Apply a coat of gesso, paint with acrylics in fun, swirling patterns, and finish with a layer of clear sealant, allowing each coat to completely dry before adding the next. To form the plates, cover dessert-size paper plates with three layers of newspaper

mache. After the mache dries, finish as you did the cups.

To make matching napkin rings, tape a strip of cardboard into a ring shape and cover it with several layers of newspaper mache. Stuff the ring shape with aluminum foil to help keep the shape. Then form flower shapes by gathering a 6-inch (14 cm) strip of mache-soaked newspaper from the center until the ends meet. Squeeze the ends together until they stick, then roll a small piece of mache-soaked newspaper into a ball and stick it in the flower's center. Hot-glue the flower to the ring after both have completely dried. ❖

Fabric Tepee

Designer Dolly Lutz Morris formed the clever base for this project with a paper plate. First fold the plate into a cone shape with a 4-inch (10 cm) diameter at its base and taped it together at the sides. Cut off the cone's top tip and then cut off the cone's bottom so it sits flat. Next, cut a 13- x 10-inch (33 x 25 cm) rectangle of muslin and dip it in fabric stiffener. Cover the cone with the muslin, turning the bottom edges up under the inside of the cone and cutting off the excess fabric at the top and in overlapped areas.

After the fabric completely dries, cut a 2-inch (5 cm) opening for the door, bend the flap back, and add motifs with acrylic paints. To add a leather look to the tepee, first apply a coat of acrylic varnish. After it dries, apply a coat of acrylic antiquing medium according to the manufacturer's instructions. To finish the tepee, secure three 9-inch (22 cm) twigs with a rubber band about 2 inches down from the top. Then push the twigs down through the top opening and secure them in place with hot glue. ❖

Pie Plate Masks

Designer Anne McCloskey used a simple glass pie plate to form a base for this fun children's project. First coat the inside of a pie plate with petroleum jelly. Apply three layers of newspaper strips that have been soaked in a mache mixture and put the plate aside to dry.

Next, sculpt ridges around the eyes and mouth with wadded-up pieces of mache-soaked newspaper. Create the raised areas of the nose and the cheeks by taping pieces of cardboard onto the mask and then maching over the cardboard. After the mask dries,

coat the entire mask with a layer of acrylic gesso. When the gesso dries, add abstract designs on the mask with a black marker and pastel blocks of acrylics. Finish with a clear coat of acrylic spray, and glue a string to the back of the mask for hanging if desired. ❖

Dinosaur Piggy Bank

Designer Tommy Woolf notes that even young children can create this piggy bank with just a little adult supervision. First cut out a piece of fabric wide enough to cover a cardboard oatmeal box. Smooth fabric stiffener onto the fabric's wrong side. Position the fabric around the container and add additional stiffener to the right side of the fabric, pressing out any air bubbles and excess stiffener with your fingers. Fold the excess fabric up under the bottom of the container and trim the top fabric flush with the container with a craft knife. Finish the container's top by gluing a circle of construction paper in place and then cutting out a coin opening with a craft knife. ❖

Easter Egg Hunt

Designer Anne McCloskey began this project with the intent of making a small bowl for her living room, but couldn't resist turning the bowl into a basket after creating the colorful finish. Begin by coating the outside of a bowl with petroleum jelly. Then apply five layers of newspaper strips soaked in a mache mixture, alternating the direction of the strips with each layer. After the outside of the basket dries,

gently remove it from the bowl and allow the project to dry for another few days. Before painting, prime the basket with a layer of acrylic gesso to prevent the newsprint from showing through. Then cut out a strip of cardboard for the handle and hot-glue it to the basket.

———

To apply the colored tissue papers, paint the backs of small tissue squares with white craft glue that's been diluted

with a little water and then press them against the basket, taking care to overlap the colors. After all of the glue dries, add highlights with a gold glitter pen, and then coat the entire basket with a layer of clear acrylic gloss.

———

Create the Easter eggs with the same techniques as the basket, using foam eggs as a base and two layers of newspaper strips instead of five. ❖

Denim Hat

Nine-year-old hat model Amanda Connolly couldn't stop giggling while her mother, Joyce, formed a mold for the hat by shaping a piece of aluminum foil around her head. While her mom was working on the hat, Amanda soaked several denim strips in stiffener and then shaped them around plastic cups to form bracelets.

After you've formed the mold, soak a large square of denim in fabric stiffener and shape it over the mold. Apply extra stiffener to the edges, and then create rolls and curves in them. ❖

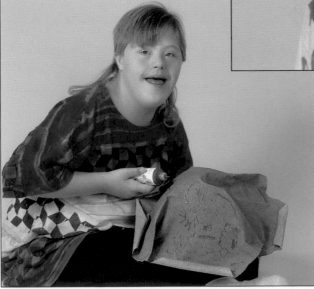

After they've completely dried, fabric hats and bracelets can be decorated with puff paints, sequins, beads, buttons, and more.

Piñatas

aura Rogers' Spanish classes at Clyde Elementary School enjoy making piñatas every year as part of their studies of Latin countries. In Mexico, piñatas are frequently made from a bamboo frame that's been covered with bright paper streamers. They are usually found at birthday celebrations, where a group of children take turns being blindfolded and try to break the piñata open. When the piñata is finally broken, everyone rushes forward to collect the candy and small toys that spill out from it.

Instead of using a bamboo frame, Señora Rogers' classes built their piñatas over balloons with several layers of newspaper strips that had been soaked in a mache mixture. Different shapes of balloons were used depending on the desired shape, and the balloons were popped after the mache had completely dried. The piñatas were then primed with a coat of acrylic gesso and painted. ❖

The points on this star burst were made by taping cones made from circles of construction paper around the balloon before macheing.

The bird's body was made by securing two different sizes of balloons together with masking tape. The nose base was formed by taping a small circle of construction paper into a cone and then taping it in place on the smaller balloon.

For this snowman, several different sizes of balloons were secured together with masking tape before macheing.

Newspaper Mache

Although instant paper-mache has become the medium of choice for most crafters, the tried and true newspaper and paste method still works just fine. Some crafters just prefer this method to instant mache, and most children enjoy the process and the mess.

Following is a list of some popular mache recipes. They all work well, and the choice is just a matter of personal preference.

1 cup of flour, 1 cup of warm water, and two teaspoons of salt

White craft glue diluted with water

Wallpaper paste diluted with water

Prepare to work by tearing newspaper into strips measuring 1 to 2 inches (2.5 to 5 cm) wide and mixing up a mache recipe. Dip each strip of newspaper in the mache mixture and then run the strip through your fingers to squeeze out any excess. Place each strip over the mold until it's covered, then repeat the process at least four or five times, alternating the direction of the strips with each layer.

After the piece completely dries, finish with paints as you would an instant paper-mache piece. (Note: A coat of gesso is especially important to prevent the newsprint from showing through in your finished piece.)

Troll Box

Crafter Tommy Woolf made this simple box as a hide-away for his son to stash his favorite treasures in. First cut out a square of fabric large enough to fit over a plastic box. Coat the wrong side of the fabric with a layer of stiffener. Fold the fabric over the container, positioning the gathers to fall at the corners. While the fabric dries, decorate the top of the container by gluing cutout troll motifs in place. ❖

Nursery Container Decoration

Designer Chris Rankin recommends this project as a quick and inexpensive baby shower gift. Begin by cutting about 1/4 yard (.2 m) of cotton fabric to fit the outside of a baby wipes container. Coat the wrong side of the fabric with stiffener. Curve the fabric around the container, folding it over the top and bottom edges. Next, apply a layer of stiffener to the right side of the fabric as you press out any air bubbles with your fingers. While the fabric is drying, decorate the top of the container by gluing cutout motifs in place. When the fabric dries, use a craft knife to trim the top fabric flush with the container's top. ❖

Animal Jewelry

Dottie Shultz fashions these animal pins from a 1- or 2-inch (2.5 or 5 cm) foam egg that has been cut in half. Dottie delights in watching the faces evolve, and the expense for these precious pieces is minimal. Smaller or larger foam eggs can be used to create button covers, pins, or holiday tree ornaments.

To form an animal face for a scarf necklace, form a loop with a 1-inch piece of medium-gauge floral wire and insert the wire into the top of the foam. Cover the foam with a thin coat of instant paper-mache, leaving the wire loop exposed.

For the cow, form the ears with two balls of mache. Form each ear over your thumb, rounding them at the top end, and then press them in place against the egg's wider end. To form the muzzle, shape a piece of mache into a heart and then press it against the egg's narrow end, centering it between the ears with the wide end of the heart facing upward. Then flatten the muzzle and form a mouth at the heart's pointy end with a toothpick. Next, make two comma strokes with the toothpick for the nostrils.

For the rabbit, form the ears from small balls of mache, taking care to create indents in their middles and to taper the ends to a gentle point.

For the face, apply additional mache to create a tapered nose, two puffy cheeks, and a ridge down the middle for the muzzle. Press in indents for the eyes.

After the animals completely dry, prime them with a coat of acrylic gesso and let it dry overnight. Then paint the animals with one or two coats of acrylics, and follow with a coat of clear matte acrylic spray after the paint dries. To create the warm appeal of the animals' faces, apply a coat of water-based antiquing medium after the spray dries. ❖

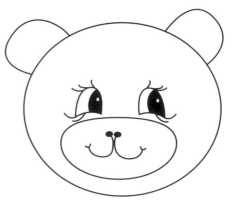

Designer Dottie Shultz uses the same techniques described on page 89 with smaller foam eggs to create button covers and pins. To form the bear's face, first cover the foam with a thin coat of instant paper-mache. Then form the bear's ears with two small balls of mache and smooth the mache together with a damp-ened bristle brush. Poke a hole in the center of each ear with the brush's wooden end, then finish shaping the ears and press them against the top of the foam.

To form the bear's muzzle, shape a ball of mache into an oval and add it to the lower part of the face, centering it between the ears. Smooth the mache together with the bristle brush, creating a curved muz-zle as you work. Place the bear on a screen rack and allow it to completely dry before painting. Prime the bear with a coat of acrylic gesso, then paint with one or two coats of acrylics, follow with a coat of clear matte acrylic spray, and antique, allowing each coat to completely dry before adding the next. ❖

Bear Basket

Avis Everett enjoys adapting her stiffened bow baskets for use in children's rooms. Avis suggests filling the baskets with Christmas gifts during the holidays or baby gifts for a shower. Stiffen the bows as directed on pages 12 and 13 and attach motifs cut out from the fabric. ❖

Fabric Ghost and Witch

Although Dolly Lutz Morris created these Halloween decorations with her kids in mind, she was surprised that so many adults liked them. Dolly used inexpensive materials that she had on hand, and tried to take extra care to make the figures' expressions friendly.

Ghost

Fill the bottom of a 22-ounce liquid dish detergent bottle with sand or pebbles to form a stable base. Press a 2.5-inch (6.5 cm) foam ball over the top of the bottle to form an indent. Remove the ball, fill the indent with glue, and replace it. Next, bend a length of 20-inch (50 cm) medium-gauge floral wire back 5 inches (12 cm) at each end to form the arms and secure the wire to the bottle by wrapping the middle of the wire around the bottle's neck. Cover the wire with masking tape to prevent it from rusting later and staining the fabric.

Next, cut out a fabric circle that's 30 inches (75 cm) in diameter. Dip the fabric in stiffener, wring out any excess, and place the middle of the fabric circle on the ghost's head. Secure it in place by pressing a rust-proof sewing pin through the fabric and into the foam ball. Place a loose rubber band around the bottom of the ball (the neck area) to hold the

fabric in place, and remove it when the fabric is partially dry.

Arrange the fabric over the arms, making drapes and folds in the body area. Turn the raw edges under and make ruffles at the bottom. Overlap the open edges that will fall from the hand area of the arms and downward. Pin them shut with pins until they dry. After the fabric completely dries, add facial features with a black marker and secure the overlapped areas with a dab of glue if necessary.

Witch

Prepare the witch's body, head, and arms the same way you did for the ghost. Then cut out a circle of muslin that's 2.5 inches in diameter and brush one side of it with white craft glue. Place the circle over the foam ball to create the face and secure it in place with rust-proof sewing pins until it's dry. Cut out the robe as directed in the sidebar on page 77. Cut the center front fold open and then stitch the side and underarm seams with a 1/4-inch (6 mm) seam allowance. Dip the robe in fabric stiffener, wring out any excess, and place it on the bottle with the open middle on the back. Turn the bottom edges under, arrange the fabric in folds, and secure in place with pins.

While the face and robe are

drying, cut out a circle of cardboard with a 4-inch (10 cm) diameter with a hole that's 2.25 inches (5.5 cm) in diameter in the center. Then make a cone from cardboard that's 4 inches (10 cm) tall with a 2.25-inch diameter base. Tape the cone together and then tape the cardboard circle to the base of the cone, folding up the brim as you work. Now cut out a circle of black fabric with a 15-inch (39 cm) diameter. Dip the fabric in stiffener, wring out any excess, and position the center of the circle on the point of the cone. Secure with pins and then gently ease the fabric down the cone. Secure the fabric at the cone's base with a rubber band. Cover the top and under sides of the rim by tucking the excess fabric inside the hat (cone).

For the hair, unbraid several 4-inch lengths of sisal rope and glue them in place. Add the facial features with acrylic paints or magic markers, and glue on the hat. Secure the hat in place until the glue dries by pressing pins through the hat and into the foam ball. Glue orange ribbon around the top of the brim and an orange bow at the neck. Finish by gluing a miniature broom in place. (You can purchase the broom in a craft store or make your own with a dowel and a section of an old cinnamon stick broom.) ❖

Halloween Mask

Designer Dolly Lutz Morris collaborated with her partner, six-year-old daughter Margaret, to make this mask. To custom-make a mask for your own child, first measure the length and width of the child's face. Cut out an oval incorporating these measurements from poster board. Then measure the size and position of the child's eyes, nose, and mouth, and mark their positions on the poster board.

Next, form a mold for the mask by building up the facial features — the forehead, nose, cheeks, mouth and chin — in modeling clay, leaving the eyes recessed. Then cover the clay with a smooth layer of plastic wrap. Cut four layers of cheesecloth that measure 3 inches (7.5 cm) larger on all sides than the mold. Dip the cheesecloth in fabric stiffener and wring out any excess stiffener. Smooth the cheesecloth over the mold, patting out any wrinkles, and tuck the cloth into the mouth area with a popsicle stick.

After the cloth completely dries, remove it from the mold and cut off the excess fabric at the sides. Hold it up to child's face to mark the exact position for the eye and mouth holes, and then cut out the eye holes and a center slit in the mouth with manicure scissors. Paint the mask with a light layer of acrylic paint that has been diluted with 50% water, and then add the features with undiluted paint. Last, stitch a length of 1/4-inch (6 mm) elastic in place, using the child's head as a size guide. Faux hair can be glued in place or the mask can be worn with a wig. ❖

Play Time Jewelry

In addition to her contemporary jewelry, Korean designer Sarah Kim enjoys making whimsical figures for children's jewelry. For these figures, roll out some instant paper-mache with a rolling pin and then use your dampened fingers to form the body shapes. Next, add more mache to form the boy's baseball glove, and then cut out the jeans and overall straps for the bear with a craft knife. After pressing the jeans and

straps in place, fold up the bottom edge of the pants to create the illusion of cuffs. For the hat, add curves and rolls to the edges of a mache circle and then add texture with the blade of a butter knife. For the angel, shape triangles of mache into wings and press them in place, then add texture with a knife. Before the mache dries, insert a paper clip into the top of the heads, leaving just enough of the hook

protruding to form a loop.

After the pieces completely dry, prime them with a layer of acrylic gesso. When the gesso dries, use a fine brush to add acrylic colors, and finish with a layer of clear aerosol sealant after the colors dry. Last, thread the paper clip with a colorful shoelace or length of fabric to form a hanger, or hot-glue a pin backing in place. ❖

TREASURES AMD TRIFLES

Lace Bowls

Tommy Wolff formed these elegant lace bowls from inexpensive, crocheted doilies. First coat the wrong side of a doily with fabric stiffener, and then place its center over the center of a plastic wrap-covered mold. Shape the sides of the doily around the sides of the mold. Brush the right side of the doily with a layer of stiffener, and reward any uncooperative areas of the doily with another layer of stiffener. After the doily completely dries, gently pop it off the mold. ❖

Lace Jewelry

For lace connoisseur Joyce Cusick, discovering fabric stiffener has allowed her to enjoy lace in a new form — as jewelry. Joyce recommends that beginners refer to an illustrated lacemaking book to master the stitches and that their first Battenberg attempts be done in white cotton thread since it's less slippery than metallic threads.

To make these pieces, arrange Battenberg tape as shown in the illustration, then add the fill stitches. Dip the finished lace in stiffener and press out any excess. After the lace is completely dry, add craft jewels and pin backings with hot glue, and add the necklace clasps for the choker. ❖

Mache Jewelry Beads

Crafter Sarah Kim sees endless design potential in paper-mache beads. The beads are quick and inexpensive to make, and can be decorated with a myriad of surface design materials. To form the beads, knead the dough until it's smooth. Break off small pieces and roll them into beads. Pierce the beads through their centers with a tapestry needle to create stringing holes. For color, add drops of water color paint to the dough before kneading it, or paint with acrylics and a fine brush after the beads dry. ❖

Rolled Jewelry

Jewelry designer Sarah Kim enjoys forming instant paper-mache into unusual shapes to create her jewelry pieces. Sarah just plays with the mache until she feels satisfied with the results, never knowing what the finished piece will look like in advance.

To form the colorful necklace and pin shown right, Sarah first separates a large ball of mache into four small bowls and add drops of water color paint. Knead each ball of mache and add additional drops of paint until you like the color. Next, roll out each ball of mache with a rolling pin, and then stack the colors on top of each other. Press all four colors together with the rolling pin. Next, tear some of the dough into triangles with your fingers, and roll some of the dough into small balls, not concerning yourself with whether the shapes are evenly sized. For the necklace, form threading holes with a tapestry needle. For the pin, press several of the shapes together, and then hot-glue a pin backing to the back side after the mache dries.

For the simple earrings shown left, roll out some mache and use a craft knife to cut out two similar-sized triangles. Roll the triangles into the shape in the photo, and press holes for the earring pieces into the tops. After the mache dries, prime the shapes with a layer of acrylic gesso and then paint them white. When the paint dries, use a narrow tip permanent marker to make vertical lines, and then insert the earring fixture through the holes. ❖

Fruitful Finds

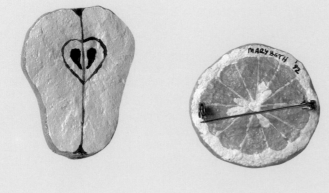

For a matching jewelry pin, shape a bead slightly larger than the necklace beads. Place an opened jewelry pin in the center of the back side and gently mold a little mache over the straight portion of the pin. After the bead has dried, paint it to match the necklace beads.

Mary Beth Ruby began making jewelry to use up little bits of instant paper-mache she frequently had left over from her large animal sculptures. To begin, shape small pieces of mache into bead shapes with dampened fingers. You can make traditional bead shapes, such as the round and oblong beads toward the ends of the necklace, or you can experiment with fruit shapes.

———

After forming the beads, poke a piece of coat hanger or other stiff wire through the center of each bead and place them on a piece of foam to dry. Turn the beads once every day until they are completely dry. Seal the beads with a coat of acrylic gesso, and paint them with acrylics, and then finish with a coat of clear var-nish, allowing each layer to completely dry before applying the next.

———

String the painted beads into a necklace, combining with stone beads if you like, and finish with a jewelry clasp at each end. If you're in a productive mood, make several extra beads for the young people in your life — they're fun to paint and virtually indestructible. ❖

No Laughing Matter

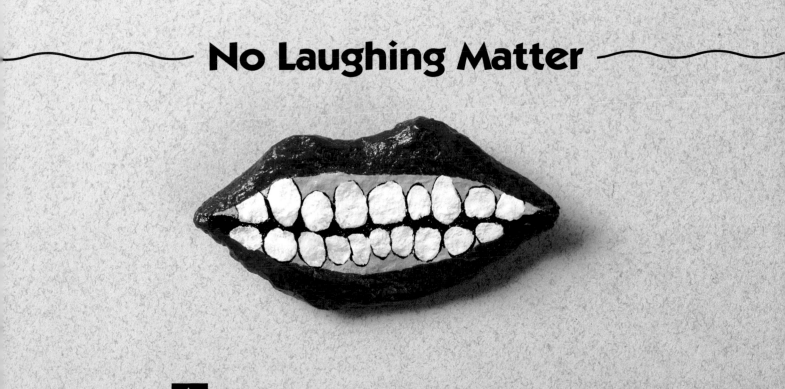

A scrap piece of instant paper mache and the errant imagination of Mary Beth Ruby created these grinning teeth. First mold the mache over a pin backing and then finger-smooth it with damp-ened fingers until you like the shape. After the mache com-pletely dries, apply a clear coat of gesso. Paint the lips and teeth with acrylics, and fin-ish with a clear coat of varnish, allowing ample drying time between each coat. ❖

Strawberry Hill

These strawberry beads are a favorite with Mary Beth Ruby's customers, and she mixes them with paper mache leaves and black onyx stone beads. These beads and the pin were created with the same techniques used on the citrus beads on page 107. For an interesting visual twist, Mary Beth curves the edges of the leaf beads upward, so they curl and roll on the necklace when they're worn. For fun variations of this project, Mary Beth likes to carve designs into the wet mache or press in interesting found objects such as feathers and stones. Separate shapes can also be made and pressed into the wet mache. (See the wall pocket basket on page 40 for an example of this technique.)

The matching earrings use the same strawberry shape and painting design, although the jewelry construction requires a little extra work. First make several twists in a short length of 20-gauge jewelry wire. (See illustration.) Insert the wire ends into the top center of the strawberry bead and gently work the mache around the wire. Add the earring wires after the bead dries and you've finished painting and varnishing. For the strawberry bracelet, form mache around an empty masking tape roll (cardboard strips taped together also work well). After the mache completely dries, prime it with gesso, decorate with painted designs, and finish with a clear coat of varnish. ❖

Fabric Flower Pot

Dolly Lutz Morris designed this project as something children could make as a gift for Mother's Day, although you may like the idea so much that you'll make several with fabrics that complement your home's decor.

Cut out a circle of fabric large enough to more than cover your chosen container. (A plastic yogurt container was used here.) Dip the fabric in stiffener,

wring out any excess, and place the center of the container in the center of the wrong side of the fabric. Bring the fabric up over the container, evening it out around the sides and securing with a rubber band 1 inch (2.5 cm) down from the container's top. Tuck the excess fabric inside the container, and use rust-proof sewing pins to hold the fabric in place until it dries.

After the fabric completely dries, glue a length of lace ribbon around the pot, allowing it to overlap by 1/2 inch (13 mm) on the back side. Tie a length of ribbon around the pot into a bow just above the lace. Then cut a piece of floral foam with a serrated knife to snugly fit inside the pot and glue it in place. Last, insert stems of dried flowers into the foam to form a nicely shaped arrangement. ❖

Glitter Jewelry

Korean designer Sarah Kim, who usually works with clay, enjoyed adding style to her instant paper-mache jewelry with glitter and fabric paints. Sarah did not try to achieve an extremely smooth surface (like her clay pieces) because she liked the textured, handmade paper look of the mache.

For the pin and earring set, above, roll out mache with a rolling pin, and then cut out a large triangle for the pin and two smaller triangles for the earrings. Cut out four more triangles, fold them to create rolls, and place them aside. After all the shapes dry, prime them with a coat of acrylic gesso and then paint them with acrylics. Sprinkle glitter over the paint while it's still wet. When the paint dries, hot-glue the rolled triangles to the flat ones, and then hot-glue the earring and pin mounts to the backs.

For the heart necklace, left, cut out heart shapes and pierce holes in them on each top side with a tapestry needle. After the mache completely dries, prime them with gesso and then paint them with acrylic colors. Outline the hearts with dimensional fabric paint, and sprinkle glitter over the wet paint. After drying, thread waxed yarn through the holes

and attach a jewelry fastener.

To form the piece shown right, knead some blue water color paint into the mache until it's very soft. Form the mache over a cardboard paper towel roll. Roll another ball of white mache flat and pull off several strips. Arrange the strips around the blue mache and press them in place. After the mache completely dries, brush on some clear craft glue and sprinkle glitter over it. After the glue dries, finish with a light layer of clear aerosol sealant. ❖

Peppermint Box

Crafter Tommy Woolf makes lots of decorative boxes from holiday fabrics every Christmas. Filled with peppermints or other treats, the boxes are very inexpensive, and allow Tommy to spread holiday cheer without spending a lot of money.

First cut out a square of fabric large enough to fit over a small metal container. (An instant coffee container was used for this project.) Soak the fabric in stiffener and wring out any excess. Arrange the fabric over the container and fold the corners up as you would if wrapping a gift package. Add a decorative roll to the top of the fabric or fold it down inside the container, adding additional stiffener if necessary. Fold the fabric over the top of the container, positioning the gathers to fall at the corners. Trim off any excess fabric after the box is completely dry. ❖

Mache Ornament

Mary Beth Ruby combines leftover scraps of pulp with found objects and her favorite decorating materials to create fun holiday tree ornaments. For the ornament shown here, cut out the shape with a knife and poke a hole for the hanger through the top. Wait for the mache to completely dry, turning it several times a day to prevent the edges from curling up.

After the mache dries, apply a layer of gesso, and paint with copper acrylics for a holiday look. Brush on a clear-drying craft glue and sprinkle glitter over it while still wet. When the glue dries, add a coat of clear varnish, and glue on a special feather. ❖

Fabric Ornaments

Crafter Sarah Kim's idea for these stiffened fabric ornaments came when she took out her box of cookie cutter forms to do some holiday baking. To make an ornament, first trace the shape from a cookie cutter onto a piece of heavy fabric. Cut out the shape and dip it in fabric stiffener. After the fabric dries, hotglue a gold hanger to the top and decorate the fabric with puff paints. ❖

Angel Bear Ornament

Dottie Shultz made this keepsake angel from just a small amount of instant paper-mache, some craft foam shapes, and scraps of holiday materials. To begin, cut 1/2 to 3/4 inch (12 to 18 mm) off the top of a 4-inch (10 cm) foam cone, and insert two toothpicks in the top of the cone. Insert a 1- to 1.5 inch (2.5 to 4 cm) foam ball into the toothpicks to create the angel's head.

Cover the entire base with a layer of mache. Then add extra mache around the bottom of the skirt and smooth it into the rest of the body. Poke a hole for the halo into the top center of the head with the wooden end of a paint brush. For the ears, form two small balls of mache and press them over your thumb to form a semicircle. Attach them to each side of the head and use a wet brush to smooth the joining areas together. To form the muzzle, press a larger ball of mache into an oval, attach it to the face, and smooth the joining areas.

To form the arms and paws, roll two tubes of mache about 2.5 inches (6.5 cm) long. Round off one end of each tube for the paws, and attach them to the body. Be sure to leave enough room between the arms to insert the miniature gift package. Then use a toothpick to form a sleeve, and make a thumb on the top of each paw. To finish the dress, smooth the surface with dampened fingers. Use a paintbrush handle to make indentations at the bottom of the skirt about 3/4 inch (18 mm) apart all the way around, then smooth the indentations into the appearance of nice fabric folds. Smooth away any fingerprints and then place it on a cake rack to dry.

After the angel completely dries, apply a coat of acrylic gesso and allow it to dry. Paint the angel with acrylics. (Some areas may need two coats.) Follow with a coat of aerosol sealant, a coat of antiquing medium, and then another coat of sealant, allowing each coat to completely dry before continuing with the next.

Form a metallic pipe cleaner into a halo with a tail. Attach the halo to the angel by dipping the tail piece into craft glue and then inserting it into the hole made during the molding process. To form the wings, make a bow with unraveled paper ribbon, leaving tails on both sides. Secure the center of the bow with a short piece of ribbon, trim the bow tails into points, and glue the bow to the center back of the angel. For the neck detailing, gather a piece of lace, fit it around the angel's neck, and tie the gathering strings together at the back. Last, lightly glue the lace at the center back of the angel and glue the package between her paws. ❖

Fabric Angel Ornament

Dollmaker Dolly Lutz Morris enjoys decorating her Christmas tree with fabric angel ornaments because they add such fun colors and patterns to the tree. To form the angel's body, bend both ends of a 12-inch (30 cm) length of medium-gauge floral wire over 2 inches (5 cm) and insert a 1/2-inch (12 mm) wooden bead through one end of the wire so that 1/4 inch (6 mm) of wire extends through the bead loop. (This extending loop of wire will later be used to form a hanger.) With the wire protruding from the bottom end of the bead, form a triangle with a 2.5- to 3-inch (6.5 to 7.5 cm) base, then twist the wire ends to secure. Place a piece of tape under the bead to keep it from slipping down.

To form the skirt, cut a rectangle of plaid fabric measuring 5 x 8 inches (12 x 20 cm). Run a gathering stitch at the neck edge (the 8-inch edge), gather to 1 inch (2.5 cm), and tie off with a knot. Dip the fabric in stiffener and wring out any excess. Place the gathered edge under the bead at the neck. Fold 1/2 inch of each side over the wire triangle on the back and turn up 1/2 inch at the bottom. Arrange drapes in the fabric and allow to completely dry.

To form the apron, cut a rectangle of muslin measuring 8 x 3 inches. Run a gathering stitch at the top, gather to 2 inches, and tie off with a knot. Dip the fabric in stiffener and wring out any excess. Position the top of the apron 1 inch below the neck and pin to secure. Fold the sides under 1/4 inch and the bottom under 1/2 inch. Arrange drapes and folds in the fabric. After it dries, glue a length of ivory ribbon in place to look like a waistband.

To form the sleeves, cut a rectangle of plaid fabric measuring 6 x 2 inches (15 x 5 cm) and sew the 6-inch sides wrong sides together with a 1/4-inch seam to form a tube. Turn right sides out and fold under 1/4 inch at each end. Dip the tube in stiffener and position its middle area at the center back of the angel below her head. Pin in place and wrap each end around the front to form the arms. Bring the arms toward the waist and arrange drapes in the tube. After the tubes completely dry, reinforce them with hot glue.

For the wings, cut two 3-inch lengths of 1.5-inch lace, gather their unruffled edges to 1/2 inch, and tie off with a knot. Dip the lace in stiffener and arrange in drapes. After the wings completely dry, glue them to the angel, starting at the top of the head and working down and around. Next, paint simple facial features and blush. Then glue on craft hair and a narrow ribbon bow. Form a halo with some gold braid and glue in place. To finish the angel, glue a small wreath between the ends of the sleeves and decorate the wreath with a narrow ribbon bow. Last, tie a 6-inch length of twine or embroidery floss to the wire loop to form the hanger. ❖

～ Tussie-Mussies ～

Garden crafter Darlene Conti enjoys stiffening her tussie mussie bouquets with the same technique the Victorians used centuries ago. To make the stiffening mixture, bring equal amounts of sugar and water to a boil, stirring constantly, and allow the mixture to cool to room temperature. Lightly wet a doily or handkerchief with water, then place it in the sugar mixture. Remove the doily and place it on a sheet of aluminum foil to dry. After the fabric is completely dry, cut a small hole in the doily's center and insert a bouquet of dried or silk flowers that have been secured at their stems with floral tape. Ribbon streamers can be tied on for added appeal. ❖

Although Dottie Shultz often works with larger projects, such as the figurines on pages 52 and 73, she also enjoys creating fanciful treasures from candy and cookie molds. Dottie enjoys creating special effects with artists' materials to make her work more realistic.

To begin, cover the inside of the cookie or candy mold with a light layer of a vegetable-based oil cooking spray. Then press instant paper-mache mixture into the mold until it's level with the outside edges. Push any mache that overlaps the edges back into the mold and then smooth the back side.

Remove the pieces from the molds by using a knife or spatula to gently loosen the edges, and then easing the pieces from the molds. Smooth out any marks made by the knife and use a toothpick to make a hanging hole in the top of the piece. Place the molds on a cake rack to dry, turning them once or twice a day to prevent the edges from curling. After the pieces completely dry, smooth away any ragged edges with a piece of fine sandpaper or a fingernail file.

For the Easter bunnies, lambs, Santa beards, and the white portions of the snowmen, apply two coats of a ceramic specialty paint that contains fine particles to produce a granite effect. After the paint dries, finish with a light layer of clear

acrylic spray.

Next, apply a coat of water-based antiquing medium to bring out detail in the pieces, and then finish with a light layer of clear acrylic spray, allowing each layer to completely dry before adding the next. Do not use the antiquing medium in places that have been painted white, since the medium can make the white areas look dirty. Attach jewelry pins or button covers to the backs with a multi-purpose adhesive cement after the paints dry. ❖

Portfolio of Contemporary Mache Artists

Bobby Wells

Multi media artist Bobby Wells began her art career as a weaver when she was a child, and although she's still passionate about traditional weaving, she's enjoying working with woven fabric in nontraditional ways. "I've always been very compulsive about my work — balancing my constant desire to experiment with the need to make a living."

The pieces shown here represent some of Bobby's more recent experiments with woven fabric. Bobby creates the pieces by first painting her woven fabrics (usually woven from a combination of rayon chenille and metallic threads) with fabric paint and then gluing down some unusual metallic or wrapping paper on top of the fabric. She then coats the piece with a liquid acrylic medium that hardens like glass. Next, she paints over the acrylic with fabric paint, using a sharpened toothpick as a brush. Flecks of metallic paper pieces are added next to finish the design, and she finishes with another coat of liquid acrylic.

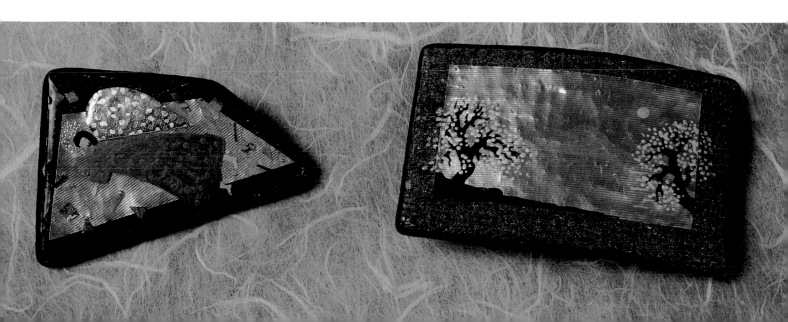

Richard Glass

"I JUST TACKLE WHATEVER COMES ALONG," SAYS MULTI-MEDIA ARTIST RICHARD GLASS, REFERRING TO THE ARRAY OF CHALLENGING ASSIGNMENTS HE UNDERTAKES FOR LOCAL ACTING AND BALLET TROOPS IN EL PASO, TEXAS. THE TWO MASKS SHOWN HERE WERE CREATED FOR THE BALLET ACT PERFORMED IN THE KING AND I. TO CREATE THE MASKS, RICHARD FIRST MADE A PLASTER HEAD AND MOUNTED IT TO A JIG SO HE COULD ADJUST HIS WORK TO ANY ANGLE. HE THEN MADE A BLACK FELT HOOD WITH A TIE CORD FOR EACH MASK AND POSITIONED THEM OVER THE PLASTER HEADS. HE FORMED THE BASIC FACIAL STRUCTURE WITH CARDBOARD AND MASKING TAPE, MAKING ALLOWANCES FOR VISION AND BREATHING. THE NEXT STEP WAS TO APPLY A LAYER OF INSTANT PAPER-MACHE.

ALTHOUGH HE HAS WORKED WITH TRADITIONAL MACHE MIXTURES OF NEWSPAPER AND PASTE IN THE PAST, RICHARD LIKES WORKING WITH THE INSTANT MACHE BECAUSE THE PAPER "IS GROUND TO A FINE PULP WHICH IS GOOD FOR

GETTING DETAILS, ALTHOUGH YOU HAVE TO ALLOW FOR SHRINKAGE AND SOME DISTORTION DURING DRYING." THE DANCERS WHO WORE THE MASKS WERE ADORNED IN LAVISH COSTUMES, WHILE THE VILLAIN WORE SIX-INCH RED FINGER NAILS RICHARD MADE BY CUTTING ACRYLIC TUBING IN HALF AND SHAPING IT WITH A HEAT GUN. "PAPER-MACHE IS JUST ONE OF MANY MATERIALS I USE. I ALSO WORK WITH JUST ABOUT EVERY OTHER MATERIAL — FIBERGLASS, WOOD, METALS, PLASTICS, FOAM, FABRIC, FUR — IT JUST DEPENDS ON THE TIMING, BUDGET, AND PURPOSE OF THE PROJECT."

Untitled masks, *approximately 14 x 24 inches.*

Photos: Evan Bracken

Mary Beth Ruby

MARY BETH ALWAYS BECOMES INTIMATELY INVOLVED WITH HER WORK. "EVERY SCULPTURE I MAKE IS LIKE A CHILD TO ME. IT STARTS WHEN I GO TO MY COLLECTION OF TUBES AND JUNK, AND BEGIN TAPING THE ARMATURE TOGETHER. I WORK ON SEVERAL ANIMALS AT ONCE, BUILDING INSTANT PAPIER MACHE OVER THE ARMATURE FORM. AFTER ABOUT A WEEK OR TWO, THE SCULPTURE IS COMPLETELY BUILT, DRY, AND READY TO PAINT. I'VE DEVELOPED MY PROCESSES ON MY OWN, HAVING HAD LITTLE FORMAL ART EDUCATION."

MARY BETH FREQUENTLY COMBINES DISPARATE FIGURES IN HER SCULPTURES, SUCH AS THE HEFTY HIPPO SITTING ON A DELICATE VICTORIAN SOFA, BOTTOM RIGHT, AND HER WORK TENDS TO RADIATE THE WHIMSICAL MOODS WITH WHICH SHE APPROACHES IT. "MY ART ROOM IS LIKE ANOTHER WORLD, A PLACE WHERE I CAN ESCAPE AND HAVE FUN, AND I HOPE MY WORK REFLECTS THOSE FEELINGS."

Top
Redheads, *24 x 20 inches.*
Bottom Right
Stripes and Spots, *14 x 17 x 12 inches.*
Bottom Left
Teen Cow, *11 x 20 x 10 inches.*
All photos: Paul Ruby

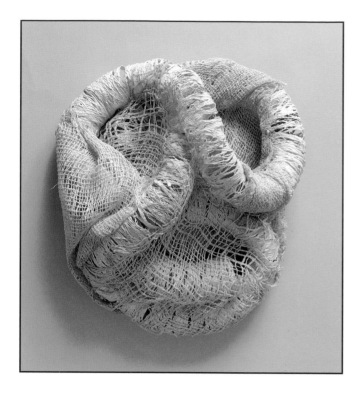

Mary Ellen Williams

ALTHOUGH SHE'S BEEN AN ARTIST FOR AS LONG AS SHE CAN REMEMBER, MARY ELLEN WILLIAMS BEGAN WORKING IN FIBER (PRIMARILY WEAVING) A FEW YEARS AGO IN AN EFFORT TO MERGE FINE ARTS WITH CRAFTS. TO DISPLAY HER WOVEN FABRICS IN THREE-DIMENSIONAL FORM, MARY ELLEN DRAPES FABRIC STIFFENED PIECES OVER CIRCUS BALLOONS.

ALTHOUGH MARY ELLEN'S BACKGROUNDS (SUCH AS THE SCREEN, BELOW) ARE USUALLY PREPLANNED, SHE RARELY HAS AN IDEA OF WHAT THE FINISHED PROJECT WILL LOOK LIKE, AND REALLY ENJOYS THE GIVE AND TAKE OF THE RELATIONSHIP.

Untitled Works, *28 inches x 36 inches, above; 36 inches x 39 inches.*
Photos: Evan Bracken

Dolly Lutz Morris

"THE FACES POSE A DEFINITE CHALLENGE BECAUSE PAPER-MACHE ISN'T QUITE AS WORKABLE FOR DETAIL AS SOME OTHER MEDIUMS," SAYS DOLLMAKER DOLLY LUTZ MORRIS. DOLLY DREW INSPIRATION FOR MARGARET, THE DOLL SHOWN LEFT, FROM THE DOLLS OF THE 18TH AND 19TH CENTURIES WHO HAD PLAIN, SERENE FACES WITH PAINTED HAIR AND EYES. DOLLY DEVELOPED HER OWN TECHNIQUES FOR ACHIEVING A MELLOW, AGED APPEARANCE IN HER DOLLS, AND SHE SOMETIMES ADDS PLASTER (AS WAS DONE CENTURIES AGO) TO THE MACHE MIXTURE TO MAKE IT MORE MALLEABLE AND INCREASE DURABILITY.

DOLLY'S MOTHER STARTED HER DOLL COLLECTION FOR HER WHEN SHE WAS A SMALL CHILD FROM OLD DOLLS RESCUED FROM RUMMAGE SALES. DOLLY'S FIRST HANDMADE DOLLS WERE CLOTH, BUT SHE EVENTUALLY BEGAN LOOKING FOR A MEDIUM WITH MORE VERSATILITY. SHE CHOSE PAPER-MACHE BECAUSE IT DID NOT HAVE TO BE FIRED IN A KILN AND BECAUSE SHE LOVES TO ADD FINISHING DETAILS WITH DECORATIVE PAINTING AND THE MACHE TAKES PAINT WELL.

DOLLY'S FAVORITE MACHE DOLLS ARE HER FATHER CHRISTMASES, WHICH REMIND HER OF THE OLD GERMAN SANTAS AND BELSNICKLES. SHE ENJOYS CREATING SOMETHING SPECIAL FOR EACH DOLL TO HOLD, AS WELL AS A UNIQUE COSTUME, EXPRESSION, AND CHARACTER. SHE NEVER WORKS WITH MOLDS BECAUSE SHE BELIEVES IT WOULD DIMINISH THE INDIVIDUALITY OF HER PIECES.

Left and Above
Father Christmas Series, *approximately 6 inches x 15 inches.*

Right
Margaret, *approximately 4 inches x 15 inches.*

All photos: Evan Bracken

Joyce Cusick

Joyce Cusick's original conception of The Travellers, left, was at least 6 feet tall. When she began thinking of the technical aspects of the project, however, she had difficulty deciding what to use for molds. "Molding the fabric over the living room furniture seemed a bit excessive," she says. Instead, Joyce made the items in much smaller scale, and borrowed items with interesting shapes from the kitchen to use as molds.

Joyce's previous sculpture experience involved glass, wood, and poured metal pieces, but she enjoys the way fabric sculptures take on a life of their own, and how easily smaller pieces can be assembled with larger ones. The fabric's texture is an important part of the finished piece, so Joyce coats only the wrong side of the fabric with stiffener. "There's a unique freedom of expression when working with lace and gauze fabrics." she says. "The fabric just seems to expand into its own relationship with space."

Top
Brides, *8 inches x 3 inches.*

Top
The Travellers, *8 inches x 3 inches.*

Photos:
Evan Bracken

Lucas Theologue Grillis Adams

"I LIKE MAKING ANIMALS THE BEST," SAYS SCULPTOR AND MULTI-MEDIA ARTIST LUCAS ADAMS, "ESPECIALLY WHEN I'M ALMOST FINISHED WITH A PIECE AND IT STARTS TO COME TO LIFE BEFORE MY EYES." LUCAS HAS BEEN WORKING WITH PAPER-MACHE FOR MORE THAN 25 YEARS. HE BEGAN WITH TRADITIONAL TECHNIQUES, FORMING CHICKEN WIRE BASES AND THEN COVERING THEM WITH STRIPS OF MACHE-SOAKED NEWSPAPER, BUT HAS BEEN WORKING WITH INSTANT PAPER-MACHE FOR MANY YEARS.

LUCAS IS THE SON OF A GREEK EMIGRANT, AND HE BELIEVES HE WAS STRONGLY INFLUENCED BY THE TIME HE SPENT WITH HIS FATHER IN GREECE ON THE ISLAND OF PATMOS WHEN HE WAS A YOUNG BOY. LUCAS SIGNS ALL

HIS ART WORK WITH GRILLIS IN HONOR OF HIS FATHER, WHO DIED WHEN LUCAS WAS TEN. ALTHOUGH LUCAS SPENDS MUCH OF HIS TIME WORKING ON MORE SERIOUS PIECES, SUCH AS THE SIX-FOOT SCULPTURE SHOWN LEFT, HE ALSO ENJOYS PLAYING WITH PAPER-MACHE. "HALLOWEEN IS SUCH A FUN TIME TO BE AN ARTIST," HE SAYS.

Top
No Arms to Hold You, *6 feet x 20 inches.*
Left
Assorted Costumes, *5-plus feet.*
Photos: Lucas Adams

Index